Out of Nazareth:

Christ-Centered Civic Transformation In Unlikely Places

Randy White & H Spees, Editors

Urban Loft Publishers

Skyforest, CA

Out of Nazareth
Christ-Centered Civic Transformation In Unlikely Places

Bakke Graduate University
An Imprint of Urban Loft Publishers

Write: Permissions, Urban Loft Publishers
P.O. Box 6
Skyforest, CA 92385
www.urbanloftpublishers.com

Senior Editors: Stephen Burris & Kendi Howells Douglas
Editor: Andrew Wood
Copy Editor: Jennifer Johnson
Graphics: Amber McKinley & Elisabeth Arnold
Cover Photo by Steve Skibbie

Scripture quotations are from the New Revised Standard Version Bible, copyright © 1989 National Council of the Churches of Christ in the United States of America. Used by permission. All rights reserved.

ISBN-13: 978-0997371772
Made in the U.S.

All profits from this book will be used directly in the training of emerging leaders in Fresno for Christian Community Development

To Fresno

And all who seek your peace

Who gather in the shade of our

Beloved Ash Tree

To imagine together

Your imminent

Flourishing

Endorsements

Fresno, now that's a special place. Fresno is on the cutting edge of what the rest of the nation is waiting to see.

-Dr. John Perkins, Founder,
Christian Community
Development Association

A lifetime of living and serving in an urban environment has uniquely prepared these seasoned co-authors to assemble wisdom that has been well tested by practical, grass-roots experience. Out of Nazareth makes a significant contribution to a much-needed body of literature to guide and inspire a new generation of urban visionaries.

-Dr. Bob Lupton, Founder, Focused Community
Strategies and author of *Toxic Charity*

For more than four decades it has been my privilege to enter cities on six continents by asking local Christian leaders a simple question: "If you had to prove that God is alive in your city, where would you take me and what would you show me to prove it?" These chapters, basically eight guided "city tours" of Fresno, provide insightful responses to my question. Moreover, the educator in me benefited by these delightful practitioners teaching me HOW they learn and not just what they know. This is the real benefit of this practical Kingdom case study in how the Gospel goes from intentional neighboring of Jesus followers over

25 years, leading to the spiritual transformation of persons, and the social transformation of public places in Fresno, California.

-Ray Bakke, Urban Historian, Theologian,
Author of *Theology as Big as the City*

Fresno offers a unique example of how to create a process of urban transformation that brings real change. Randy White, H. Spees and their co-authors explain innovative ways residents in Fresno -- churches, the business community and local government -- collaborate in the ongoing transformation of their community. This is must-reading for urban workers, church leaders and college or seminary students who want to join those on the creative edge of community transformation.

-Tom Sine, Founder, Mustard Seed Associates,
author of *Live Like You Give a Damn!*

Something good has come out of Fresno. It is called transformation. Real, sustainable, Christ-centered transformation. From being famous for its dereliction to being famous for its radical restoration, the story of Fresno California is a remarkable one. White and Spees bring to us in this book hard-earned lessons in civic transformation which can be adapted and repeated in your city.

-Scott Bessenecker, Director of Mission,
InterVarsity Christian Fellowship

It's all about community! This inspiring new book

reminds us that we cannot love our cities well until we know them. Out of Nazareth offers real-world advice from a diverse set of seasoned practitioners who are living out their theology daily, bridging the issues that divide and polarize, and demonstrating the power of faith-centered connection. A necessary resource for anyone wishing to effectively strengthen the communities they love.

-Dr. Lauren Speeth, Elfenworks Founder and author of *Intelligence & Compassion in Action*

God does extra-ordinary things in unexpected places and this book highlights this amazing fact. In a broken and divided world, it's refreshing to read about acts of transformation, unity, and empowerment.

-Efrem Smith, President and CEO of World Impact and author of *Killing Us Softly*

Movements that make a difference are collectively provocative and individually helpful. Out of Nazareth is the story of such a movement. The best practitioners -- those who are actually changing the world -- rarely find time to devote to putting their story in writing, so it makes sense that in a collaborative city movement, many practitioners would collectively tell the story. Grounded in biblical theology and best practices, Out of Nazareth serves as a blueprint of cross-domain city transformation and instantly becomes part of the required reading list for anyone engaged in community transformation.

-Eric Swanson, Leadership Network. Co-author of *The Externally Focused Church* and *To Transform a City*

As someone raised in Fresno County, I have watched with interest the transformation in the city of Fresno. Now we can read about this work of Shalom through various lenses, using both theoretical and narrative perspectives. The chapters weave together the story of God's work in Fresno, demonstrating what God can do in the unlikely places of the world.

-Jude Tiersma Watson, InnerChange, Associate Professor, Fuller Theological Seminary

For those who long for their city's flourishing and possess the desperation to do what it takes to realize it, this book offers an inspirational field guide. Fresno is a must-know case study for community transformation and this book lifts up the hood to see the moving parts.

-Wes Furlong, Evana Network

Fresno's story of civic transformation is a shining example of how good people from diverse backgrounds can see crisis as an opportunity to set aside differences and come together for positive change. Out of Nazareth, Fresno's (ongoing) story, is an inspiration and a road map for Christ followers with a heart and mission for civic transformation.

-Eileen Kooreman, Urban Leadership
Development Advocate

The way that I pastor and lead my church in D.C. is shaped by the beautiful years I spent in Fresno. Every policy maker I disciple and every sermon I preach contains echos of H and Randy's influence on me. The District Church's vision to be a church for the city of Washington, D.C. has its origins in the Fresno soil.

-Rev. Matthew Watson, The District Church,
Washington, DC

Can anything good come out of Nazareth (where the savior of the world grew up and was shaped by living in obscurity and by a hard life working in construction)? This sentiment has often been expressed about poor day-laborers and farm workers living in Fresno, CA. Over the decades that Randy White and H Spees co-labored in the Central Valley, they demonstrated that when we live alongside those on the margins, in places others might consider insignificant, we learn that God often uses our brokenness and faithfulness to pour out his mercy, grace and justice in such a way that brings about Kingdom transformation. I urge anyone who has a heart for vulnerable places and people to read this book carefully.

-Noel Castellanos, President, Christian
Community Development Association and
author of *Where the Cross Meets the Street*

Fresno is a quintessential example of a community making progress through an intentional Christian Community Development strategy. This unique book is a multi-sector view of just how it is being done from mature practitioners. It will be a great help to those applying CCD principles across the country and around the world.

-Coach Wayne Gordon, CCDA, Pastor, Lawndale Church

Out of Nazareth is filled with humble, authentic voices that tell the story of a city that comes back from the brink. Randy White, H. P. Spees, and their contributors merge a passion for their city with a vision and strategy to bring the healing that Fresno has experienced to communities around the country. The book mines from their vast experiences to offer hope and advice for churches, nonprofits, businesses, and governments to work together for transformation. Read, be blessed, and get inspired to become a catalyst for change in your community.

- Brian Fikkert, Co-author of *When Helping Hurts: How to Alleviate Poverty Without Hurting the Poor...and Yourself.*

Table of Contents

SERIES PREFACE

Urban Ministry in the 21st Century is a series of monographs that addresses key issues facing those involved in urban mission whether it be in the slums, squatter communities, *favelas*, or in immigrant neighborhoods. It is our goal to bring fresh ideas, a theological basis, and best practices in urban mission as we reflect on our changing urban world. The contributors to this series bring a wide-range of ideas, experiences, education, international perspectives, and insight into the study of the growing field of urban mission. These contributions fall into three very general areas: 1. the biblical and theological basis for urban mission; 2. best practices currently in use and anticipated in the future by urban scholar/activists who are living, working, and studying in the context of cities; 3. personal experiences and observations based on urban mission as it is currently being practiced; and 4. a forward view toward where we are headed in the decades ahead in the expanding and developing field of urban mission. This series is intended for educators, graduate students, theologians, pastors, and serious students of urban mission.

More than anything, these contributions are creative attempts to help Christians strategically and creatively think about how we can better reach our world that is now more urban than rural. We do not see theology and practice as separate and distinct. Rather, we see sound practice growing out of a healthy vibrant theology that seeks to understand God's world as it truly is as we move further into the twenty-first century. Contributors interact with the best scholarly literature available at the time of writing while making application to specific contexts in which they live and work.

Each book in the series is intended to be a thought-provoking work that represents the author's experience and perspective on urban mission in a particular context. The editors have chosen those who bring this rich diversity of perspectives to this series. It is our hope and prayer that each book in this series will challenge, enrich, provoke, and cause the reader to dig deeper into subjects that bring a deeper understanding of our urban world and the mission the church is called to perform in that new world.

Kendi Howells Douglas and Stephen Burris,
Urban Ministry in the 21st Century Series Editors

Introduction

Randy White

Can anything good come out of Nazareth?

John 1:46

It was the case of a nice theory being murdered by an ugly gang of facts.

P.G. Wodehouse

After twenty-five years of immersion in Christ-centered community development efforts in Fresno, California—the most amazing and perhaps unlikely of laboratories—two contradictory things have become abundantly clear to me. First, true community transformation requires expert skill-sets in a broad array of particular disciplines. And second, unfortunately, there *are no experts*. So I guess that means we are in trouble, right?

Well, we *would* be if what we meant by *expert* is someone with it all figured out, someone with nothing left to learn, someone who gets paid to offer opinions. But we don't. What we mean is more akin to someone who has paid the price, felt the pain of failure, the fog of confusion, and the glimmers of hope that appear along the way in the journey of seeking the abundant community. Someone who has engaged in trial and error and has seen the occasional successes rise from the rubble, who has seen the landscape changing in ways that require we start again with whole new approaches. We mean those who have abandoned the false vision of the lone ranger or the programmatic fix or the savior riding in on the white horse. We mean those who have bound themselves together to bring their specialized skill sets to bear on our most intractable problems, problems vandalizing the shalom of God in our community. It's taken some time to realize it, but we are waking up to the fact that, out of our desperation, we have cultivated just such a group of leaders. Turns out, in the midst of the concentrated poverty of Fresno and the Central Valley of California, in a place known more for raisins and "why would you live there?" jokes, we are rich in that human asset. Can anything good come out of Fresno? The same question has been asked of many cities. But the *facts* might surprise you.

What follows in these pages represents the hard-won perspectives of those actively engaged in a Christ-centered process of seeking the transformation of their community into a place of abundance and peace. But they also speak of the lessons born of the blood, sweat and tears of the arena. It represents the real-time efforts of leaders who are still in it, fighting every day to live out the Gospel in ways that redeem and restore and bless-valuing theory, but being real about the facts faced on the ground. It's a story of what's working, told by practitioners.

Dr. H Spees served with John Perkins in Mendenhall, Mississippi, and is a founding board member of the Christian Community Development Association. He has led youth organizations, health care clinics, leadership foundations, and community transformation efforts across the U.S. and internationally. His chapter on Christ-centered civic transformation, based on best practices that have emerged here and around the world, sets the stage for the entire book.

In addition to being an editor of this book I have had the privilege of thinking about community transformation through the lens of movement dynamics, observing and understanding how they are cultivated in cities among emerging leaders, a phenomenon we have seen grow in Fresno over the last two decades. An emerging leader movement has taken hold in our city with many twenty- and thirty-somethings eagerly taking onramps to mechanisms that lead to community transformation. It has been my privilege to take initiative with this movement, and the perspective of this chapter grows out of that stewardship.

Bryson White is a gifted leader with a strong theological mind and a talent for organizing communities across ethnic and class lines to address systemic forms of injustice and build coalitions that have clear and proactive goals for change. His chapter on that subject reflects that balance of history, theology and practice in a way that brings a timely and important insight to the process given the things we are facing nationally and regionally.

Dr. Cathleen Lawler travels the world as a veteran mission mobilizer and equipper, but closest to her heart is the knitting together of local churches to understand and serve their communities through the power of multi-sector alliances in the city.

Pastor Yammilette Rodriguez holds the dual role of urban pastor and executive director of a Community Benefit Organization focused on equipping youth for ministries of justice in communities. She describes practical projects her youth have designed to confront gun violence, the influence of alcohol and liquor stores, and a political process that too often disregards the voices of the next generation of leaders, as well as specific, bedrock values and approaches that practitioners must deploy.

Professor Jacob Huang uses his sociology insights and knowledge of technology to help pastors and practitioners get to know their communities in ways they may have ignored, placing data in service of transformation. These new tools will equip churches and institutions with the data they need to get beyond the guessing and anecdotal stories that often inform strategic decisions about the needs, profiles, and assets of the communities they serve.

Monika Grasley pulls from her long history and current involvement in transformative actions in her community to explore the power of an asset-based approach to catalyzing change, anchoring her perspective in real-time examples and the reflection that emerges from them. As the director of a Community Based Organization, experience has been her powerful teacher, and we get to be her companions and co-learners on the journey.

Finally, Pastors Phil and Rici Skei put forth an amazing case study of a church that has centered its reason for existence in a particular geography, and take us on the journey with them as they fall in love with it, serve it, are transformed by it, and, are transforming it in deeply spiritual, physical, relational, political, and hope-filled ways. You will never forget the stories they tell and the unique structure of their church as seen in this chapter.

There is much we have left out. We have not discussed the movement in our city toward a built environment that honors community or transforms neglect into a renewed sense of place. We have not explored at length the political decisions that strengthened the core of our city and the momentum generated by the faith-rooted community transformation movement that helped it along. And we have not attempted to describe the searing challenges we still face as we seek the beloved community that welcomes immigrants and treats equally every specific-ethnic group that calls this place home. These deserve serious treatment, but are beyond the scope of this project. However, this is a book that is rooted in our experience, as imperfect and flawed as it is, an experience that has made clear progress in seeking the peace of the city.

If it takes a village to raise a child, it certainly takes a dedicated community to catalyze transformation in the name of Christ in a city. Our hope is that this glimpse at the work of a few of those on this catalytic team, and the insights that have been hard won by them, might be of encouragement and some practical help to you and *your* team, as you seek the peace of your city. We certainly agree on a set of values, and a theory of change certainly plays a part. But these insights and stories emerge from practitioners. While we don't offer this as a model, we do offer it as one example of a journey of transformation, one that is in fact fruitful, and one that we are joyfully on together.

Randy White
Fresno, California

Chapter One

Peace for Cities

Christ Centered Civic Transformation

H. P. Spees

Director, Strategic Initiatives, Office of the Mayor, Fresno, California

Seek the peace and prosperity of the city.

Jeremiah 29:7

Peace doesn't happen without a fight. The best fighters fight out of pain. As a recent candidate for mayor of my city of Fresno, I received help from the builder of a new, local boxing gym. I called The Builder to thank him and he told me of their new, state-of-the-art facility in the heart of our downtown. I yelled downstairs to my wife, "Get your sweater, baby. Let's go watch some boxing!" That night we met Gilbert and his wife Lourdes, the operators of the gym. Gilbert credits boxing with saving him from the streets and from prison. Now he returns the favor to kids in our town. He gave us a tour of the gym, and the last stop was at the 16-foot ring. On the wall next to it was a picture. "That's my sister in her military uniform. After two tours she was killed by her husband in a murder-suicide. This ring is dedicated to her; it's where we offer free self-defense classes to women—so no woman in our city will ever have to be a defenseless victim of domestic violence" (Sheehan, 2015, 1).

Gilbert and Lourdes are in hand-to-hand combat for the peace of Fresno. Their pain presses them into the fight to transform our city kid by kid, woman by woman. *Their* fight makes *me* want to fight beside them.

This book is full of fighters, women and men who have taken the fight for the soul of their city seriously but in radically different ways ... some through church planting and youth development, others through community organizing or nurturing a culture of institutional and organizational collaboration, one through data and analysis. But with every one you will feel the fight.

The Longing for Peace in Our Nation and World

As we fight against the threats in our world, there is no question there is a growing and palpable longing for peace in a world trending toward trouble and violence. Just a decade and a half into the 21st Century it is obvious to all that threats and conflict are on the rise. It is the summer of 2016, a summer where we in the US have witnessed a pattern of fatal tragedies which seem to alternate weekly, from shootings of unarmed citizens by police, to shootings of law enforcement officers themselves, in a see-saw of violence. This year's Summer Olympics, a global symbol of peace, have been marred by the violence between Rio de Janeiro's 85,000-member security force and the gangs in the many favelas. Fourteen people have died during the two weeks of the games (Watts, 2016, 1). Add the number of assassinations by lone wolf shooters or the mentally ill and suicide bombers and you have the makings of a new wave of fear, and an even greater longing for peace (Pearle, 2016, 1).

Gun violence, gangs and terrorism are not the only factors driving this thirst for peace. There are negative global trends that in the long term could be even more troubling to our social stability, including increasing economic disparity (Stone, Trisi, Sherman and Hornton, 2016,

1). increasing religious hostility and increasing mistrust in institutions, especially religious and police institutions (Jones, 2015, 1).

Peace for Cities: The 21st Century's Global Urban Challenge

But as much as everyone wants peace in every community, there is a particular need for peace in our cities. Perhaps the most significant trend in our world is urbanization. For the first time in human history, as of May 2007 there were more people living in cities than in rural areas. One hundred years ago only 5% of Americans were urban dwellers; now more than 80% of Americans live in cities (Leadership Foundations, 2011, 2). According to the United Nations, 54% of the worlds population resides in urban areas (WUP, 2014, 55). By 2050, over two-thirds of humanity will be city dwellers (Hanlon, 2007, 1). Cities are becoming the dominant social reality of the 21st Century, eclipsing even states and nations in their importance to humanity's future.

Downside

The downside of urbanization is that fueled by trends in violence, disparity, religious hostility, and institutional mistrust, cities can become the catch basins of human misery. "Urban centers are grappling with a dizzying array of serious social issues, exacerbated by shifts in job markets and a shortage of decent housing." (Hillis, 2007, 2). The rise in slums is one of the most disturbing realities today (United Nations Human Settlements Programme, 2003, 6). "Cities are unquestionably the new door through which the world becomes either a place of peace and prosperity or a place of violence and scarcity." (Hillis, 2007, 2).

Upside

But there is also an upside to urbanization. Dave Hillis, President of Leadership Foundations, a global organization committed for over 50 years to working for peace by reducing poverty, crime and violence in over 70 cities around the world, envisions a hopeful future for cities: "Despite their impediments and deficiencies, cities are the primary vestibule of promise and potential to become, as Dr. Martin Luther King described, the 'Beloved Community.'" (Hillis, 2007, 7). Cities can be a critical gathering point where talent can be mobilized and resources leveraged to reverse trends and set new ones.

Even as troubling trends drive conflict and the longing for peace upwards, Hillis sees a spiritual phenomenon emerging, what he calls "a strong, growing movement among people of good will and good faith joining forces to take seriously Christ's call to the City. That call is simple: To heal broken lives and hearts so that healthy people are living in healthy places." (Hillis, 2007, 2). We call this movement in cities "Christ-Centered Civic Transformation."

The Urban Soil that Grew this Book

Before we look at the elements making up an action framework for Christ-Centered Civic Transformation (CCCT), we think it is crucial to acknowledge that, ultimately, the strategic actions of one who fights for the peace of their city must emerge from the soil of their city. If they don't, they are not worth your time—just throw them on the stockpile of ideas and theories that someone wrote out of the comfort of an office or from a political party more concerned with winning than serving, or from the safe distance that academia can at times afford.

This book is rooted in the soil of Fresno—and a hundred other cities—systemic and structural challenges result in personal pain, stunted life and premature death. Why Fresno? Does it seem unlikely? In CCCT, context is essential. Every city has its own fingerprint and deserves its own tailor-made responses. What good can come up out of your city's soil? As you get your hands dirty in the soil of your city, you join a growing fellowship of urban practitioners, people of good faith and good will, who are discovering each other and sharing what they are learning from their cities as they attempt to flesh out a love for their city that transforms her geography of pain into a community of peace.

Defining Christ-Centered Civic Transformation (CCCT)

There is a movement of thousands across the country and globally, seeking the peace of their cities. And although it is God's Spirit and truth that joyfully animates and motivates this movement, there are a number of philosophical, theological, political, and practical components that provide a framework for CCCT as a basis for action. We can discover them by looking closely at the four key elements of CCCT: its *object*, its *goal*, its *heart*, and its *approach*.

First, the *city* is the object of CCCT, the context in which the Spirit is raising up this movement. Second, *peace* is the goal of CCCT, a profound peace best described by the biblical term *shalom*. Third, *Christ* is the heart, the center, the values core of CCCT, most visible in the Incarnation. And fourth, *transformation* is the measure CCCT uses to judge whether the power in sectors and institutions, in families and churches and neighborhoods, is in fact being unleashed in ways that lead to positive change in our harshest urban environments and flourishing throughout our city.

These four elements working together as Christ-Centered Civic Transformation give us a framework for action that can help us become what our cities desperately need: *Transformational Urban Leaders*.

Pursuing peace with Christ's heart for our city will not only change our cities, but will change us as well.

And, by the way, although our focus is on the *city,* urbanization is causing rural and village realities to experience urban problems as well, which means many of these same principles work when applied to villages, towns, and rural communities.

The City is the Object

Because the City is the object of Christ-Centered Civic Transformation, how we *see* the city is crucial. Transformational urban leaders see the city uniquely in three ways: we see the city out of our desperation; we see the city as a gift of God; and we see the city as common good community.

Seeing the City Out of Our Desperation

One city's story has given hope to many in the US as much because of the desperate situation its citizens faced as the hopeful outcomes they achieved. In the early 1990s, Fresno, California, the capital of the world's most productive agricultural region, the San Joaquin Valley, woke up from being a somewhat sleepy, family-oriented farm community to being a full-blown, California urban reality with all of the problems associated with the inner city. The fifth-largest and the fastest-growing city in the state, Fresno suddenly found itself with a population of close to a half million people and the highest per capita rates of violent crime of any city in the state in every category but murder. I even overheard local leaders joking darkly that Fresno's Chamber of Commerce would go to bed praying for Oakland to maintain its number one ranking in homicides.

Those in the most vulnerable neighborhoods lived the crisis long before those in the secure, predominantly white neighborhoods became awake to it. But when a young Anglo man from Hanford, a small community in an adjoining county, was murdered while Christmas shopping at Fresno's biggest mall, and when a Labor Day shooting spree saw gang members stop, rob, and shoot people on a circuit that began and ended in the Southwest section of Fresno but included the Northwest, Northeast, and Southeast districts, the feelings of fear and the sense of "out-of-control-ness" became universal. That year there were 128 gangs identified with 8,000 validated members, 13,000 car thefts, and 100 homicides. Fresno was losing its soul.

Then, the Rodney King trial sparked the LA riots on April 29, 1992. Joseph Samuels, Fresno's Chief of Police, would reveal that even as LA burned, his officers were practicing anti-riot tactics and maneuvers at the fairgrounds, so seemingly inevitable was the forecast of violence for Fresno. What was happening? We as leaders were being forced to see how our city was self-destructing.

When Leaders Choose to Get Desperate

At that point, two pastors, Bufe Karraker and GL Johnson, both in their seventies, both respected leaders of large, predominantly white churches, called a meeting of about 12 diverse business, church, law enforcement officials, and elected leaders at San Joaquin Country Club. "What can be done?" was the singular question. There was no answer.

A second meeting took place. John Perkins, noted Christian community activist, had been flown in. His message: "Listen to the people in the most vulnerable neighborhoods. Build relationships that lead to reconciliation. Jesus is as much about justice as he is about evangelism. The church can be a resource, but only if it is authentic in its commitment to do whatever it takes over the long haul *with*—and not just *for*—those living closest to the problems." Again, the question: "What can we do?"

The Chief of Police spoke up. "I don't know what you are going to do," said Samuels. "But before you do anything, I want you as leaders to do a ride-along with my officers on a hot Friday night. It's summer. Crime is up. You need to see what we see every night." With that challenge, the "Cops and Clergy Ride Along" was organized. That night I witnessed the death of a young man, shot in the head with a handgun at point blank range. I was riding with Officer John Ferretti. It was the last call for service to come up on the patrol car's computer screen: "Party out of control. Shots fired." The address was Northwest Fresno—a part of town where this level of violence was unexpected. After arriving, I followed Ferretti past the yellow crime scene tape and a million yellow Dixie "kegger cups" strewn on the ground in the panic. The first thing we saw in the backyard was the fence pushed down by what must have been a stampede of kids, then at our feet, on the patio, a 17-year-old boy, twitching, because he had been shot point blank in the head with a .25 caliber handgun. He was dying. We had beaten the paramedics. A girl, noting the clergy collar I was wearing—we all had been asked to wear collars—grabbed my elbow. "Father," she pleaded. "Would you please pray for Deandre?" Stunned, in shock, I found voice, my prayer praying through me in a stream of heartbroken words for Deandre, for my kids— at that moment he was my kid, too—and for every kid in Fresno...all were at risk.

The next day, we met at the Fresno Rescue Mission. We debriefed. Many stories, similar to mine, were shared. There were moments of silence. Short bursts of prayer. What was happening? We were seeing, feeling, and owning the pain in our city. And God was using that to make us desperate.

What would we do? We would stay desperate together and meet each month, but not at a set time. Instead, we would meet by invitation of the leaders who found themselves in charge of systems that were overwhelmed and whose hearts were broken because of the pain and destruction they witnessed.

So we met in the closed-down wing of the juvenile hall. We met in the chain link enclosure that was the exercise yard on top of the jail. We met in the board room of the school district that had tried three times to pass a bond measure without success. We met on 17 acres of land given to Habitat for Humanity in West-Fresno, our most disenfranchised community. And 40 pastors and ministry leaders from various ethnicities and denominations met in the mountains above Oakhurst for three days and two nights, crying out to God and listening to how he would lead us.

At one point, we felt like we were getting some traction, some focus. Politicians began requesting to come and speak to our meeting. We told them, "No. . . come for prayer; come to be a part. This is not a political forum." Someone suggested that we form a nonprofit organization with a 501 (C) 3 tax-exempt designation. But an older, wiser head said, "No! The moment we name this and organize it we will think we've done something, and there is so much that needs to be done, we can't afford to think we've done anything." So our gathering became known as the "No Name Fellowship." Our mission: "Releasing God's Resources through Reconciled Relationships to Rebuild Our City." We developed a liturgy for each meeting around three-E's: Expose ourselves to the pain of our city; Exchange data and information on strategic interventions; and Engage in some tangible, constructive way forward. There were some early wins. The juvenile court judge, Lawrence O'Neill, invited No Name to meet in the closed-down wing of the juvenile hall. It had been closed as a part of county budget cuts. The judge's opinion was that with juvenile crime out of control and the need never greater for youth accountability, closing the wing had been a very bad idea. Within months the wing was reopened and No Name exercised its influence along with a newly-established Fresno Business Council to get plans for a proactive juvenile boot camp approved as well.

In another win, Chuck McCulley, superintendent of Fresno Unified School District, the fourth-largest district in California with close to 80,000 students, invited No Name to visit and see what classrooms were facing. No Name got behind a bond measure process that had failed several times, made a video called "5 Holy Minutes" about the need for strong schools, and the measure passed by 77% of the vote. It was the largest measure of its kind in California history.

Roger Minassian, Senior Pastor of Pilgrim Armenian Church, had never met a gang member in his life. But after hearing that people in LA were so filled with despair they were burning their *own* neighborhoods, he confided that he felt God calling him to resign his pulpit and start a nonprofit helping gang youth solve their economic problems by finding employment. He started Hope Now For Youth, and over the last 16 years Hope Now has helped over 2000 gang youth find steady employment.

The Fresno Police Department threw open the doors to partnership with churches in many neighborhoods and through many prevention and intervention activities. Their chaplaincy swelled in numbers during these times. And Deputy Chief Darrell Fifield, with the help of Alan Doswald and Gordon Donoho of Evangelicals for Social Action, designed a unique program called Care Fresno. This program asked the owners of high-density, crime-infested apartment complexes to donate use of a unit, asked a church to voluntarily staff the unit as a family resource center, asked the local school to provide guidance for mentoring and tutoring, and asked the police department to stay connected after breaking up drug and gang activity. The result: a 65% drop in calls for service in 15 to 20 apartment complexes.

A movement of young leaders moving into inner-city neighborhoods was inspired by World Impact and fueled when InterVarsity leaders Randy and Tina White formed the Fresno Institute for Urban Leadership offering housing and internships for college students in Fresno's inner-city. This resulted in a continuous flow of relocators into key, vulnerable neighborhoods.

A number of these early wins sparked a movement that continues today, with the faith community right in the middle of it.

From Last Place to All-American City

It would be inaccurate to say that everything that happened in Fresno was the result of faith-based activity. Leaders in every sector— teachers, cops, business owners, and literally thousands of others—joined in with renewed vision for a renewed city. Much credit was given, however, to what took place in and through the Church. And looking back, there is consensus that the community's desperation was a major driving force. The results were measureable in terms of crime reduction, neighborhood development, the emergence of a more participatory civic culture, and a new hope for downtown revitalization. One crescendo was the awarding in 2000 of the All America City Award to Fresno by the National Civic League, eight years after the LA riots. Later, a new mayor, Alan Autry, would run and win on a platform that characterized these years: "Changing Fresno from a Tale of Two Cities into a Story of One Community." Tim Stafford, Senior Writer for *Christianity Today*, summarized four positive factors leading to an expanded role for the Church in Fresno's renewal. He said,

> "Fresno's story is very different. Dozens of leaders in dozens of institutions are involved, with dozens of styles, so there's no one model, no single leader. The church in Fresno is all over the map, literally and figuratively. It's premature to say that what's happening in Fresno will make a lasting difference...Nevertheless, in talking to many of those leaders, I came away believing that the story in Fresno is worth our attention, precisely because it requires rethinking what is normal for the church in America today." (2000, 48)

Here are the **Four Factors** Stafford described that set the Fresno story apart:

1) *Organizations Promoted Cooperation.* "First, two respected Christian organizations (Evangelicals for Social Action and Fresno Leadership Foundation) promote cooperation for the good of the city, and particularly for the good of the poor. It's rare to find such strength in groups that exist simply to encourage and to catalyze others. The long, good history of ESA and the dynamic, trusted leadership of FLF bring people together in common purpose."

2) *Prayers and Trust Building Crossed Barriers.* "Second, for years pastors from many denominations have prayed together and built mutual trust. It's something when an African-American pastor like Paul Binion, who takes a somewhat cautious view of white evangelicalism, can say, 'I know all the players and they know me. When we don't agree, we can duke it out and still love

each other. Racial reconciliation is not the end, it's a means,' Binion says. 'Just because we can get along doesn't mean we've arrived.'"

3) *Faith Leaders in Government and Churches Led.* "Third, seasoned Christian leaders in government and in some of the best-known churches in town led the way. No Name Fellowship served as a bridge for them to share concerns. Again, Paul Binion: 'Leadership at this level must come together and decide to do it. They must intentionally decide to have an interest in our city.'"

4) *Desperation became a Force for Change.* "Fourth, desperation forced the city's leadership to change. 'I think many cities have never reached that critical need,' says Jim Westgate, a professor at Mennonite Brethren Biblical Seminary. 'We could no longer ignore our problems. They were just out of control.' That operated from the government side as well. 'Institutions that had kept Christians and Christian institutions at arm's length really denied themselves the generosity and fervor of Christian people in problem-solving,' says Mayor Jim Patterson. 'For the community as for the person, when we've tried everything, we finally went to God.' (Stafford, 2000, 8)

Twenty-Four Years Later

The legacy of those desperate years is still felt in Fresno. Yes, the economic recession of 2008 took its toll. Yes, crime is increasing with the demographic bubble of the most crime-prone ages, 14- to 24-year-olds, beginning to swell. Yes, California has reduced parole requirements, dumping convicted felons back into communities to address prison overpopulation. Yes, many of the federal dollars that were available in the early 1990s are now going toward anti-terrorism. Yes, the Ferguson riots and the Black Lives Matter movement are impacting Fresno as well. But people from the church community and community at large have, over the past twenty-four years, continued to come together to address the issues. The following chapters document much of this work. Dynamic inner-city churches are being planted. The Every Neighborhood Partnership has linked churches and ministries with over 50 under-resourced elementary schools in town. Recent mayor, Ashley Swearengin, has extended the call to the faith community to be involved in new and exciting ways.

The job of Christ-Centered Civic Transformation is never over. But one lesson rings true: Desperation, at any stage of the process, has been a great friend to leaders who yearn to see their city healed.

Seeing the City as a Gift from God

As important as it is to see the city through its pain and desperation, a deficit or problem-oriented approach alone will never get us to transformation. According to John Perkins, "Cities are a gift from God," and God is actively working through people to connect the resources of faith, civic renewal, and incarnational work in neighborhoods in order to see cities socially and spiritually renewed." (Hillis, 2014, 4). The concept of the *City as gift* flows from a theology of God's providential common grace (Benedetto and McKim, 2010, 195). God created cities with the purpose of human flourishing. "Seeing our cities as God's playgrounds," according to Dave Hillis, "where we can see God's redemptive Spirit already at work in myriad ways, inviting us to join in and share our gifts, rather than as battlegrounds, where divisions create rivalry and there is dissipation and discord, is the perspective required to bring us and our cities closer to God's peace" (Hillis, 2014)

32

This positive view of city as a gift of God's common grace lends itself to all of the significant disciplines that build on the assets of a city in pursuit of its good, including Asset-Based Community Development (www.abcdinstitute.org), Appreciative Inquiry (https://appreciativeinquiry.case.edu), Community Organizing (www.rclinthicum.org), and Christian Community Development, (www.ccda.org), to name a few. You will see these at play in the chapters of this book.

Keeping Common Grace Institutions Working for the Common Good

In giving cities, God in his grace provides two things: *resources to sustain* humanity, and *government to restrain* humanity (Benedetto and McKim, 2010, 196). Through CCCT practitioners and many others who are working for the social and spiritual renewal of cities, God works to keep common grace institutions of the city working for the common good. In fact, it was John Calvin's view that because church and state performed separate functions in civil society, one of the Church's functions is to call the state's civil government to high standards concerning equity, justice, and concern for the poor (Benedetto and McKim, 2010, 195).

Seeing the city as God's gift for everyone comes with a price for CCCT practitioners: it is "the eternal vigilance which is the price of liberty" (Berkes, 2010, 1). It is staying at the task of consistently stewarding the city so that its resources are distributed and its restraints are applied in ways that benefit everyone.

Seeing the City as Common Good Community

If seeing the city at the point of its desperation *compels us to heal* our city, and if seeing the city as a gift of God *calls for us to be stewards* of our city, then seeing the city as "common good community" *shows us how to engage* our city. Every city is made up of a complexity of systems and structures. The *sectors and institutions* of a city house these systems and structures. Seeing how these sectors and institutions function together (or not) helps us know how to engage our city in ways that build it as a community for the common good. How does the church fit into this complex picture of the common good community?

The Common Good Community

The concepts of "community" and the "common good" are vital to an understanding of democratic society. It begins with balancing the tension between individual and community rights and responsibilities.

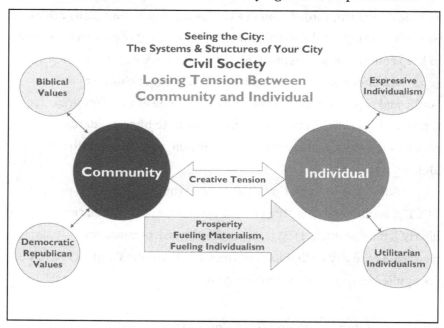

The large bubbles in this diagram illustrate this tension and balance between the interests of the individual and the interests of the community. These issues, described in the 1990s best-seller *Habits of the Heart,* one of the most thorough evaluations of American democracy, are at the heart of every city and every society. The small bubbles indicate historic streams of thought feeding both sides of the polarity, with Biblical values as one stream feeding America's value of community.

Based on this evaluation, we in America find ourselves in crisis and losing our balance. The bigger context of why our cities and families are falling apart is that this tension between the individual and the community, at least in America, has been overbalanced on the side of individualism. Ironically, our prosperity has fueled materialism which has increased individualism and depleted community. This out-of-control individualism and the decline of community has resulted in increasing disparity between rich and poor, decreasing morality in the face of unparalleled prosperity, with attendant epidemics of family brokenness and personal addiction.

The authors of *Habits of the Heart* sum up our current predicament with a reference to John Winthrop's sermon *Model of Christian Charity,* where he describes the "city on a hill" that they hoped to establish in Salem, Massachusetts. "Delivered on board ship in 1630 just before the Massachusetts Bay colonists disembarked...in that sermon Winthrop warned that if we pursue 'our pleasures and profits we will surely perish out of this good land.'" Rather, what Winthrop, paraphrasing the Apostle Paul, tells us is that

> we must entertain each other in brotherly affection, we must be willing to abridge ourselves of our superfluities, for the supply of others' necessities...we must delight in each other, make others' conditions our own, rejoice together, mourn together, labor and suffer together, always having before our eyes ... our Community as members of the same Body, (XXV).

As researchers, the authors of *Habits of the Heart* conclude that "under the conditions of today's America, we are tempted to ignore

Winthrop's advice, to forget our obligations of solidarity and community, to harden our hearts and look out only for ourselves. In the Hebrew Scriptures God spoke to the children of Israel through the prophet Ezekiel, saying, 'I will take out of your flesh the heart of stone and give you a heart of flesh' (Exek 36:26). Can we pray that God do the same for us in America today" (Bellah, Madesen, Sullivan, Swidler, Tipton, 1985, 1996, XXV).

Urban leaders pursuing Christ-Centered Civic Transformation are attempting to live out the answer to the prayer of those researchers. Here's what it might look like:

In this scenario, the push-pull between individualism and community is mitigated by God's people, who work as practitioners for the common good by rebuilding human community. CCCT at its core is committed to building the common good community through connecting people with each other, their institutions and, ultimately, God.

The Four Sectors

With that big picture showing us what we are up against in our culture as we rebuild human community, how do we start and where can we find a handhold for civic transformation? One very practical way is by seeing how the sectors of a city function together.

When most people think sectors, they think of two: public and private. But for those engaged in the actual hard work of transforming cities, there are four: the Public, Private, Nonprofit, and Community Sectors.

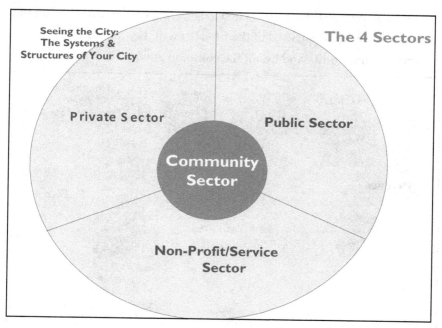

The Institutions

The first three sectors, Public, Private, and Nonprofit (Shipley, 2012, 1) all have one thing in common: they are made up of institutions or organizations. These are denoted by the squares on the diagram below.

These three sectors exist to serve the people of the city. In fact, the very purpose of institutions in a city is rooted in serving every person in the city, denoted by the community sector and its placement at the center of the diagram. This purpose is fulfilled when each institution is connected to every neighborhood in the city in coordination with every other institution in the city around a shared vision of health for the city. This is clearly the ideal. The reality is that institutions, like people, can and often do pursue their own agendas, operating competitively or on the basis of a Darwinian "survival of the fittest" mentality that can undermine community and derail the common good.

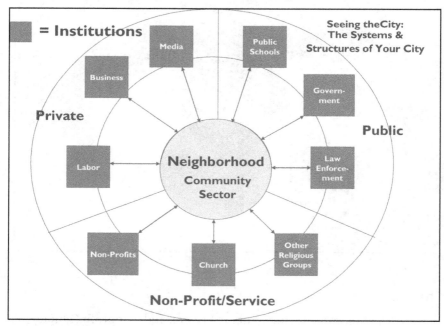

The Community Sector

The fourth sector, the community sector, is often the most neglected and misunderstood but the most important sector for those seeking the transformation of cities. The community sector is described by John McKnight, founder of Northwestern University's Asset Based Community Development (ABCD) Institute: "Those relationships formed by consent and manifested as care are the center of community. It is this consenting care that is the essence of our role as citizens. And it is the ability of citizens to care that creates strong communities and able democracies" (McKnight, 1995, ix). "The community is the site for the relationships of citizens. And it is at this site that the primary work of a caring society must occur" (McKnight, 1995, x)

In short, the community sector is important because it is where people live and where people care for each other. In a city, the community sector is found in neighborhoods, the place where people experience quality of life...or not. (McKnight, 1995, ix). It is here that the fundamental groundwork for what McKnight calls a caring society happens.

> If [the community sector) is invaded, co-opted, overwhelmed, and dominated by service-producing institutions, then the work of the community will fail. And that failure is manifest in families collapsing, schools failing, violence spreading, medical systems spinning out of control, justice systems becoming overwhelmed, prisons burgeoning, and human services degenerating. (1995, x)

Where the other three sectors are made up of institutions, the community sector is made up of what civil society scholars call "mediating institutions," those local, voluntary connections that make up a healthy neighborhood. These include the local neighborhood watch group, a block club, the PTA, families, congregations who see the neighborhood as their parish, the local school, and small businesses.

39

Together, they all make up the fabric of mediating institutions that connect people in care and communication.

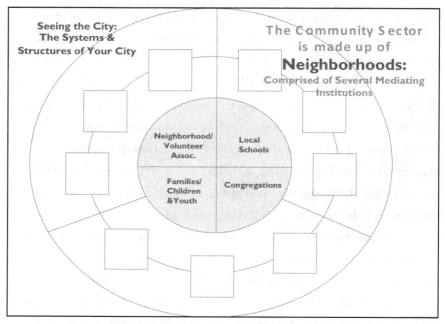

This "associational life" of a caring community or neighborhood was what Alexis de Tocqueville described as one of American democracy's great strengths: "Americans of all ages, all stations of life, and all types of disposition are forever forming associations. . . In democratic countries knowledge of how to combine is the mother of all other forms of knowledge; on its progress depends that of all the others" (deTocqueville, 1835, 185).

What happens when neighborhoods in a city become either disconnected or unhealthily dependent on the institutions of the city? What happens to the quality of life in a city's neighborhoods when these bonds of community evaporate? What happens when the mediating institutions, the human connectivity derived from rich associational life, are absent, driven out by cycles of poverty and neglect, and replaced by generational institutional dependency on welfare and other systems, entrenched crime, gangs, drugs, widespread unemployment, broken families, and fatherlessness?

Every City is a Ladder

Every urban minister can answer this question in personal terms, with deeply moving stories of the human toll taken among those doomed to live in such desperate neighborhoods. But from a systems point of view every city is a ladder. The ladder is the sum total of the neighborhoods in the community sector. The rungs are its neighborhoods, smaller areas like those served by a local elementary school. In my city, the top rung is the Forkner Elementary Neighborhood. The bottom rung is the Lowell Elementary School Neighborhood. America or any society does not make a promise that we can all live on the top rung of the ladder. But what America does promise is that we can get to the ladder.

Seeing Your City: The Systems & Structures of Your City

Every City is a ladder.

Each rung is an elementary school neighborhood. Cities can be rebuilt one neighborhood at a time.

Almost every American is an immigrant...or the daughter or son of an immigrant. That means almost every American has poverty, need, and desperation somewhere in their family tree. And that means somewhere along the way, one of our mothers or fathers or both simply took America up on its promise, got to the ladder, jumped as high as they could, reaching as far up as they could, grabbed a rung, and held on. Over the years they may have even slipped down a rung, or crawled up two and slipped down one. But they hung on, and allowed us to climb up on their backs to reach to the next rung. And that's how most healthy cities work. A city doesn't work when it doesn't make good on its promise—when people living within its borders can't get to the ladder. This describes what it is like for people living in neighborhoods characterized by concentrated poverty. These are families whose rungs of the ladder are submerged in the muck and mire of generational welfare, gangs, drug use, and neglected housing. These are adults and children living in neighborhoods rarely visited by a priest or teacher or city council member or someone fully employed or even a cop. These are kids growing up in what has become a permanent underclass.

Not only can they not move up the ladder—they can't get to the ladder, so they have no hope. And that's dangerous, for the kids, for the adults, and for the city. It's dangerous because hopelessness leads to havoc; having nothing to lose means everything else that everyone has is at risk. It means the city is at risk. And these dangerous environments are on the increase nationally and globally; a 2010 UN report found that 200 million people have escaped slums but the overall number of people in the slums is still rising.

If the bottom rungs of a city's ladder are left under muck and mire, they can rot and cause the whole ladder to feel unsteady, or tilt, or even topple. A city feels unsteady when its people are constantly hearing about dropout rates and gang violence on the evening news. A city experiences tilt when larger and larger percentages of a city's budget are

42

drawn out of development line items and into crime fighting and graffiti abatement and public housing rehab. A city topples when a flash point like the beating of a crime suspect sparks a riot.

Transformational urban leaders know their ladder, they know each rung by name, and they join together in making a commitment to the lowest rungs because by rebuilding the fabric of community within them and by reconnecting them to the institutions designed to serve them, they will not only help those living in those neighborhoods but they will also improve their whole city. By lifting the lowest rung back to solid ground, they've moved the whole ladder.

A Healthy City is a Connected City

A healthy city, then, is one where there is a common vision for the common good that is shared among its institutions (see the circular arrows on the diagram below) and where that vision is connected to the aspirations, hopes, and health of every neighborhood, (see the inward/outward arrows on the same diagram.)

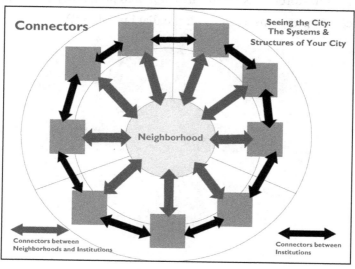

This takes connectors—individuals, networks, and organizations committed to building the city into a common good community. The alternative is institutions pursuing their own self-interests, disconnected from an increasingly alienated community, and an everyone-for-himself competition between neighborhoods.

Where Does the Church Fit?

The Church is salt and light, working for its city to become "a city on a hill." The Church achieves this stance only through understanding its complex, multi-sector relationship to the city. The Church is at its best when, through its hundreds of individuals scattered through every sector and institution and neighborhood, it permeates the systems and structures of a city in a spirit of sacrificial service.

So where does the Church fit in the multi-sector reality of the city? First, it is present in every neighborhood in many forms from Cathedrals to storefronts, from thrift stores to pregnancy care centers and recovery programs. (See #1 on the diagram above.)

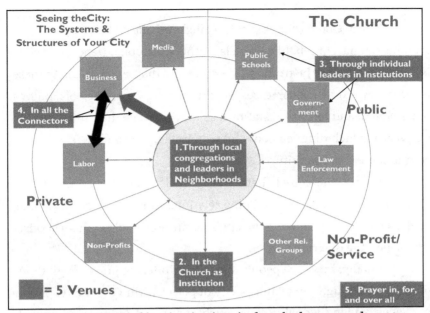

Second, it is itself an institution, in fact the largest and most complex institution in most cities. (See #2 on the diagram above.) What other organization has hundreds of branch offices? Granted, many of those branch offices are ignorant or neglectful of each other or even in competition with each other. But when a critical mass of the congregations and ministries and religious institutions in a city connect and speak with one voice, there is great potential for serving the common good and the peace of the city both practically and prophetically.

Although there are hundreds of congregations and ministries in most cities, as an institution, the church should best be placed at the bottom of the chart, to indicate our commitment to follow the servant posture and incarnational nature of Jesus (Phil 2:1–11). This strategic servant position reflects the upside down kingdom in the context of the city: that which is last shall be first and he who would lead must be the servant of all. This counteracts other triumphal views of the Church in the city which are ultimately unhelpful in the work of civic renewal.

Third, God has strategically called and placed his people, members of his church, like Daniels, Esthers, Josephs, Deborahs and Nehemiahs in every institution (see #3 on the diagram above). As these leaders steward their businesses, government agencies, schools, unions, newspapers, and television stations, as they leverage their influence for all everyone including the poor and vulnerable, they build their city into a common good community.

Fourth, there are believers in every city, called to be and functioning as connectors, building relational, structural, and systemic bridges between and among the city's institutions and neighborhoods. (See #4 on the diagram above.)

Finally, there are people and groups offering prayer at all times of the day and night, in a multiplicity of places within every city, praying in concert and individually, consciously connected and not, but divinely orchestrated to spiritually influence the city for good. This resource can never be underestimated. (See #5 on the diagram above.)

Jesus died in his body so we could be forgiven, reconciled, and connected with him forever. He placed us in his Body, the Church, so that we, becoming arms and legs, eyes and ears to each other, could become his physical replacement working for the social and spiritual renewal of our city.

There is nothing more relevant to transforming a city than the transforming power that comes from a relationship with Jesus Christ when we function as God's corporate strategic partner to replicate Jesus' presence in a city, where we can transform its people and places from disconnected geography into common good community.

The city is our object. We see the object clearly when we see our city through its pain and desperation, when we see our city as a gift from

God, and when we see our city as common good community. Now, having seen our city, what's the goal?

Peace is the Goal

Peace is the goal of Christ-Centered Civic Transformation. But peace is not cheap. Peace defined only as an individual, internal spiritual experience is not the goal of civic transformation. In Fresno we've discovered that peace in race relations is not when tearful, even sincere white men ask forgiveness of black men in a conference setting and then go back to business as usual without any ongoing relational or social justice outcomes. But peace appears when long-term relationships are forged between pastors, community activists, residents, and law enforcement officials across racial, cultural, and class boundaries in ways that provide a foundation for regular access and communication, accountability, transparency, and trust.

Peace is not quiet. Peace defined as the absence of conflict— especially when externally imposed by force—will not transform a city. Real peace is the difference between the quiet of martial law after a riot versus the deep, though imperfect, peace forged through the Truth and Reconciliation Commission hearings, a court-like process that restrained violence by restoring trust and justice after the abolition of South African apartheid in 1994 (Truth and Reconciliation Commission, n.d., 34).

Working for peace in cities means playing in the heavy traffic of complicated and diverse global urban environments. It demands understanding the interplay among sectors, institutions, and communities and the complex differences that fuel conflict. It calls for building collaboration between competing organizations, connecting, allocating, and using a wide variety of scarce resources in ways that achieve measureable, sustainable quality-of-life results in lives and neighborhoods, fairly and equitably.

Working for peace in cities involves risk like convening a summit of gang leaders discussing a cease fire; or leading a church full of Polish workers in Gdansk, Poland to declare Solidarity against Communist repression (Ingleton, 2015, 1); or respectfully redirecting a group of "Black Lives Matter" marchers attempting to shut down a state highway, as D.J. Criner, an African American pastor, did a few weeks ago in Fresno, heading off a confrontation between 300 protestors and 20 highway patrol officers in full riot gear. But as complicated or risky as it can sometimes be, working for peace can also be simple, as simple as seeing old folks sitting on their porches while children play in the street.

During a time of great pain, disharmony, and exile when Jerusalem, the city whose name means "peace," laid in ruins, God inspired one of his prophets to paint a picture of peace so simple and yet so practical that future generations would be captured by its vision: "This is what the Lord Almighty says: Once again men and women of ripe old age will sit in the streets of Jerusalem, each with cane in hand because of his age. The city streets will be filled with boys and girls playing there" (Zechariah 8:4–5).

Shalom: A Simple Yet Comprehensive View of Peace

According to this elegantly simple, Spirit-inspired snapshot, peace is when the very old and the very young, the most vulnerable persons on the chronological spectrum of a city's total population, are healthy, happy, and safe together, on their own city streets. But this simple picture of peace implies a community engaged in a complex set of actions. To see kids and seniors delight together in the safe streets of their city requires an urban environment where all of the systems and structures of the city are working together for everyone all the time and no one is left out; where leaders and the resources they steward in education, business, law enforcement, government, faith communities, and health care are all pulling in the same direction for the benefit of all the people of the city, especially for the most vulnerable and those at the margins.

Peace for cities is when everything works for everybody all the time and no one is left out. Peace is God's goal for our cities.

This vision of systemic and structural peace makes people and families and neighborhoods whole. The Biblical concept of "Shalom," the Hebrew word for peace, fortifies this vision because "Shalom" means the experience of wholeness, a comprehensive, positive relationship between God and humans and between humans and each other. This peace manifests spiritually, economically, politically, socially, including the institutions, organizations, congregations, and communities that shape people's lives. "*Shalom* is the substance of the biblical vision of one community embracing all creation," writes Walter Brueggemann, in *Living Toward A Vision*. "It refers to all those resources and factors which make communal harmony joyous and effective" (Brueggemann, 1982, 14).

Peace works as a goal for cities when defined in a way that instills hope while still facing and addressing their harshest urban realities. Hope grows when we see that "There is in the Bible a vision of what it is that God wants for God's human creatures—a vision of what constitutes human flourishing and of our appointed destiny. . . . It is the vision of *shalom,*" according to Nicholas Wolterstorff, who builds a definition of peace around justice based on rights, acknowledged by others, lived out in right relationships with God, fellow human beings, nature, myself, and finally resulting in delight (Wolterstorff, 2004, 22–23).

This type of tough peace whose final destination is delight takes hard work. In Fresno, we have to work hard to build community in under-resourced neighborhoods and fight for every inch of progress against crime, poverty, and violence. The tough work of peacemaking requires a definition of shalom gritty enough for the power struggles, inequities, and injustices of the City, but also grounded in the central, core convictions of biblical faith.

Informed by the time he spent in base Christian communities in the Philippines, Perry Yoder rejects a notion of peace that focuses on calling the victims of injustice to passively resist violence. "Peacemaking involves active opposition to and transformation of the structures of oppression and exploitation. Credible peacemaking needs substantial displays of action which directly address the problems. Through direct, visible action, witness can be given that peace and nonviolence are not a cop-out. It is this dimension of sustained and serious effort for change which I find an essential part of the biblical notion and message of peace."

Peace based on the Bible's definition of shalom stands strongly against injustice and oppression, confronts and changes unjust systems and structures, stands with victims against oppressors, and ultimately seeks to transform society (Yoder, 1997, 6). Rather than defining peace as avoiding violence, CCCT practitioners engage the systems and structures that keep people down and off the ladder that stands at the center of every city ... the ladder to freedom, achievement, and delight (Yoder, 1997, 5–6). As Perry Yoder says,

> Our world sees peace as the avoidance of violence which is maintained by force. This view is in tension with the biblical view of peace – *shalom* as the abolishment of the structures of oppression and violence. Shalom, biblical peace, is squarely against injustice and oppression ... Shalom demands a transforming of unjust social and economic orders. Rather than

being a message addressed to victims, shalom acts against oppressors for the sake of victims. In the Bible, shalom is a vision of what ought to be and a call to transform society. (1997, 6)

Peace—not cheap but simple, not overly personalized but institutionalized, not passively hoped for but actively fought for—peace is the goal of Christ-Centered Civic Transformation, a goal with the power to focus our actions even as it transforms us and our cities.

Christ is the Heart

Jesus Christ is the heart of Christ-Centered Civic Transformation and the incarnation is at the heart of Christ. All of our strategies emerge from there. But Christ is the heart and core of our values and methods not because CCCT conforms to a systematic theology or a biblical principle, but because like Jesus the Christ himself, CCCT is *incarnational.* We are people who, like him, have skin in the game. Jesus Christ was the Word that "became flesh and blood, and moved into the neighborhood" (John 1:14, The Message Bible). His mission was hands-on, leading to a level of personal transformational encounter that was directly, invariably, and intrinsically linked to a transformational encounter with society. In walking with Jesus Christ while living and working alongside people in the cities we serve, we as CCCT practitioners become transformational urban leaders partially because we, like Jesus, touch ground. As we adopt his grounded, incarnational mission as our own, we represent Christ in all that we do, anchoring the identity, methodology, and strategy of our urban transformational work in Christ's presence in us and through us. Christ's heart led to his incarnation. As we follow him into our cities, the Incarnation connects personal and social transformation in ways that release power for both, resulting in authentic, sustainable change in us and in our cities.

51

From Mother Teresa living among the dying in Calcutta; to Dr. Henley Morgan, a businessman who moved his family and businesses into the Trenchtown area of Kingston, Jamaica and now employs over 150 residents; to John and Vera Mae Perkins, leaving a middle-class life in California to return to a segregated and violent Mississippi in the 1960s and becoming grandparents to a movement of women and men relocating their homes and churches into under-resourced communities around the world; to Father Greg Boyle's Homeboy Industries planted in downtown Los Angeles, offering opportunity and a way out to hundreds trapped in gangs; to Jember Teffera, the wife of the former Mayor of Addis Ababa, and her comprehensive development of multiple neighborhoods in Ethiopia's capital city through education, health care, housing, infrastructure, and business development; to Bob Lupton, developing strategies of "gentrification with justice" in Atlanta and beyond, the past 50 years have seen hundreds of multi-generational, multi-cultural, multi-sector Christ-followers moving into, staying put in, or returning to tough urban environments with their homes, churches, ministries, and businesses. And these expressions of the Incarnation have changed individual lives, families, neighborhoods, and institutions in cities around the world.

For over 30 years, this type of gritty, Christ-following, strategic work has been lived out in my city of Fresno to the point where today the 22 neighborhoods identified by the Brookings Institute for their "concentrated poverty" have become strategic focal points for investment by congregations, students, social enterprises, and the city government itself.

Incarnation as Creative Tension

CCCT practitioners describe their mission and ministries as *incarnational.* For instance, as leaders around the US began to establish organizations—called leadership foundations—in the late 1970s to work for both the spiritual and social renewal of their cities, "what became clear was the deep sense that whatever change was to be envisioned for a city would have to be rooted in the Incarnation" (Hillis, 2014, 52).

What this meant to them was that the things most essential for their work were all grounded in Jesus's teaching about the Kingdom of God and His incarnational work in the world, where, for a city's people, "the task is to embody—literally become—the answer to the question the city is posing" (Hillis, 2014, 52).

Dave Hillis, president of Leadership Foundations, maintains that effective work in the city, in all its Kingdom dimensions, "called forth and sustained an incarnational people whose primary mission was to bear witness to the Kingdom of God in the city." A mission such as this "would hold in *creative tension* the person *and* work of Jesus with equal force and integrity—to both affirm the ideas of Christ *and* the way in which those ideas are worked out" (Hillis, 2014, 50).

As with Jesus so with us; this creative tension is at the heart of the Incarnation and so

> involves the redemption of places *as well as* people. It touches the body *and* the soul. It demands righteousness *and* justice. It calls forth personal transformation *and* systemic change. It is holistic *and* radically inclusive. It intentionally crosses boundaries: cultural, ethnic, social, economic, and religious. It is particularly concerned for those people and places that have been wrongly labeled the unredeemable least, last, and lost. In short, it is the whole gospel, for the whole church, for the whole city (2014, 50).

Incarnational Mission Among the Last, Least, and Lost

In addition to creative tension, there are three ways that the work of CCCT expresses the power of the Incarnation. Ross Langmead, in a study called "the first to define the meanings attached to incarnational mission across a variety of Christian traditions," (Langmead, 2004, cover), presents us with three ways of thinking about *incarnational mission* as 1) following Jesus's pattern; 2) participating in Christ's presence; and 3) joining in God's cosmic mission of enfleshment (Langmead, 2004, 8–9). One way to see Jesus Christ at the center of CCCT is to see how each of these three dimensions of incarnational mission show up in CCCT's work among the last, least, and lost of society.

With Children, the Last

Who are "the last?" In many ways, they could be considered the powerless in society, the voiceless, those who have no vote. Many have chosen children as the group most considered as "last" (Eberstadt, 1995, 3). Almost all CCCT practitioners work with children and youth because they intuitively see that children are voiceless, "the last" and most vulnerable in their communities. They also see them as the future, so they focus efforts on children and youth through programs ranging from providing preschool, to making sure kids are at reading level by third grade, to Urban Young Life, to mentoring the children of incarcerated parents, to providing shelter and education to homeless street youth, to a Children's Movement in Fresno that measures all public policies by how they impact children and youth.

In Matthew 18:1–5, Jesus seems to affirm that children are last by juxtaposing them to the "greatest." All three of Langmead's dimensions of incarnational mission are at work in this passage. First, as we follow Jesus's call to "welcome" children; we follow Jesus's *pattern of ministry* because He welcomed children. Second, because we, as believers, have the Spirit of Jesus resident in our lives, we represent or become *the presence of Jesus* to those children we welcome. Third, because whoever welcomes a child in Jesus's name "welcomes me," he said, we actually open ourselves to experience *the enfleshment of Christ* in the meeting.

With The Poor, the Least

Who are the "least?" In Matthew 25:34–40, Jesus makes it clear to his disciples that the least are the hungry, the thirsty, the stranger, the unclothed, the sick, and the imprisoned. Today's CCCT practitioners are motivated by Jesus's concern for the poor. This is expressed in terms of both direct service—rescue missions, prison chaplaincy, health outreach, food banks, and clothes closets—but also by addressing systemic issues such as mass incarceration, availability of affordable housing, and public policies related to payday lenders, blight, slumlords, racial profiling, and health disparities in communities of color.

Here among the least, as with children, we see again that all three dimensions of incarnational mission play out as we respond to the "least of these brothers and sisters of mine" among us. We simultaneously follow *Jesus's pattern of ministry*—Jesus spent more time with the poor than anyone else (Harvey and Goff, 2004, 287), we represent or become *the presence of Jesus* to those with desperate need; and we *encounter Christ himself in the flesh* as we experience his close identification with the poor, how what we do for them is done "for me." That the incarnational act of caring for the poor will be, according to Christ, rewarded with the assurance of experiencing His presence in the coming Kingdom adds even more significance to these sacred encounters.

With those Searching for God, the Lost

Finally, who are "the lost?" As Jesus commissions his followers in Matthew 28:18–20, he sends them and us to those who are without the good news, those who run the risk of never finding the transformational personal connection to the God of peace. "Go," he commands, and we go into our cities. As we engage the lost who have yet to encounter Christ, in the same way as welcoming children or caring for the poor, we find ourselves experiencing the heart of Christ through all three dimensions of his incarnational mission.

For transformational urban leaders engaged as CCCT practitioners in their city, every encounter—whether with a cop or teacher, a Mayor or community activist, a coach or tutor, a developer or a homeless person on the street, a gang member seeking a job or a business owner offering one—becomes sacred as our work takes us before all nationalities, cultures, sectors, communities, ethnicities, and geographies in our city. Through the work he inspires in us, we offer every person the opportunity to see the living Christ. Freed from following a formula or script, we share the good news incarnationally, *following his pattern, representing his powerful presence*, knowing that he is *enfleshing himself in and with us* in every relationship, every encounter: "I am with you always."

The Incarnation and Unity for the Sake of the City

The Christ-centered heart of CCCT as revealed in the Incarnation has powerful implications. First, it allows us to live creatively with the inevitable tensions inherent in every urban environment. Then as we, like Christ, lay down our lives for the people in our city—especially the last, least, and lost—we individually and together as Christ's Body live out his pattern of ministry, experience his presence in our work, and see him enfleshed in those we are called to serve and serve with. Finally, as we experience Christ at the center of our work and life together, we become, and we attract others to become with us, the *one* body of Christ—*one* with the triune God who is *uniting* the fragmented Body of Christ in our cities. Jesus prayed that we, his followers "may be *one*, Father, just as you are in me and I am in you. May they also be in us." As our *unity* begins to fulfill the answer to Jesus's John 17 prayer, we at times see the promise attached to that prayer come to pass: "... so the world may believe that you have sent me" (John 17:21).

Christ is the heart of CCCT. The incarnational nature of our work allows us to not only follow His heart, His values, His pattern, and His strategy, but to also encounter his heart in us, in front of us in the people we serve, especially as we share life with children, the poor, and the spiritually searching. Living out Christ's incarnational mission carries with it its own rewards—the bonds of community that form when we do things *with* people rather than *for* people, the power and transformation that come when we encounter God and access his power in our work and lives, the unity that we foster in our city because of our ability to live creatively with tension, and the joy in seeing friends and neighbors of good will consider for themselves the possibility of faith in the true and the living God.

Transformation is the Approach

Transformation is the measure of Christ-Centered Civic Transformation. The fact that measuring change is even on the radar screen of this movement is an indication of the seriousness with which it views its task. It also reflects the severe pragmatism of the city.

CCCT is transformational in four main ways. First, transformation is implicit in how it defines its target, seeing the City through the lenses of desperation, as a gift and not a curse, and as common good community. Second, CCCT practitioners measure transformation in terms of quality of life, expressed practically as kids reading by the third grade, or percentage increase in homeownership in an inner-city neighborhood, or reduction in police calls for service, or reduction in infant mortality rate among persons of color, or the elimination of a food desert. Third, CCCT is transformational because it measures change from the bottom up rather than the top down. Trickle-down economics may work as an ideology, but CCCT practitioners believe that quality of life among the poor and vulnerable becomes the ultimate measure of both biblical justice and the success of the city itself. Finally, CCCT is transformational because it measures the distribution of power, whether the power in sectors and institutions, in families and churches and neighborhoods, in classrooms and businesses is in fact being unleashed and shared in ways that lead to positive change in our harshest urban environments. Who has access to the table? And when there are leaders of good faith and good will being engaged to tackle the toughest challenges in their city, are they building the capacity of all partners together? Are they getting stuff done on the ground?

Transformation Stories

The fact that transformation is the *measure* of CCCT shows up in the stories generated by its practitioners. Here are three.

Fresno: What would it mean to change the course of a city from urban sprawl to sustainable development of core neighborhoods? It happened in Fresno over the course of the last 8 years. Ashley Swearengin, elected Mayor in 2000, became convinced that our city could not be healthy without a healthy downtown. Convinced that one of the main reasons she was elected was to care about the poor, she chose a public policy approach to addressing the disparity and poverty in our city. Building on the work of faith-based and community-based nonprofits and churches who had pioneered very local efforts in specific neighborhoods, she led the charge to pass a 2035 General Plan that redirected 45% of the City's development dollars to interior neighborhoods left behind by decades of northern sprawl. This was backed up by a new zoning ordinance and development code, the first in 65 years, and the opening up of a failed downtown pedestrian mall to through traffic. One hundred million dollars in 2015 with $100 million more on the books in 2016 indicate that market forces have agreed with her visionary direction which, if ultimately successful, will set the stage for increased home ownership and jobs in under-resourced neighborhoods, a vibrant downtown business district, and a general rise in property values throughout the city—not very sexy in themselves but of staggering significance in a town gripped by some of the highest rates of concentrated poverty in the country.

Chicago: What would it mean to connect all the resources of the city to all the neighborhoods, even those at the bottom? It happened in one Chicago neighborhood. *The Great American Millstone* is a 1986 book written by the staff of the *Chicago Tribune* documenting life in one of the most violent and unlivable neighborhoods in Chicago. One of the most hopeful stories of transformational urban leadership is the story of Pastor Wayne Gordon and Lawndale Community Church, a group of folks who relocated to this neighborhood and over 30 years joined with neighbors in a dramatic story of Christian Community Development that has resulted in a vibrant church, hundreds of new homes, a health center seeing over 250,000 patient visits a year, and the birth of economic enterprises. If you move the bottom rung up from under the mire to solid ground, you change the whole city (Gordon & Flame, 1995, 5).

Pretoria: What would it take to keep blacks from exercising retributive justice and whites from fleeing an economy dependent on their continued investment after the fall of apartheid? Stephan de Beer knew growing up in Pretoria, South Africa, that apartheid was evil. So when he went to seminary, he and some fellow students started a home for homeless black street boys. Pro-apartheid forces in collusion with the police department burned down the home, killing six of the boys. Stephan, broken and discouraged, came to the US and discovered Leadership Foundations, a network of faith-based civic intermediaries establishing organizations that coordinated faith and community-based multi-sector investment in cities to overcome poverty, crime and violence. He went back to Pretoria and talked five major congregations into funding the startup of what is now the Tshwane Leadership Foundation (TLF). After the initial fall of apartheid, there was a demographic wind shear and Pretoria moved from 95% white to 87% black in three years. Today, TLF manages hundreds of affordable housing units, provides care to homeless women and their children, incubates social enterprises, and turns slums into subdivisions. TLF was and continues to be a major factor in keeping the peace in the capital city of the country. CCCT transforms people and places, socially and spiritually.

In this first chapter, we have taken a deep dive into the four elements constituting Christ-Centered Civic Transformation: The City, object of CCCT; Peace, goal of CCCT; Christ, the heart of CCCT; and Transformation, the measure of CCCT. In the chapters that follow you will hear from CCCT practitioners who are fighting for the transformation of their city through disciplines ranging from asset-based community development to developing social enterprises, from church planting to community organization. Our prayer is that as you hear the stories of their training, their conditioning, the strategies they've developed, and the battles they've won and lost, you will find hope as you count the cost and take your stand in the fight for your own city's transformation.

Works Cited

Bellah, Robert N., Madesen, Richard, Sullivan, William M., Ann Swidler, Tipton, Steven M., (1985, 1996) *Habits of the Heart Individualism and Commitment in American Life*, introduction to the updated edition by The Regents of the University of California (Berkeley: University of California Press, p. xxxv.

Benedetto, Robert and McKim, Donald K., (2010), *Historical Dictionary of the Reformed Churches,* 2nd ed. Lanham, MD: Scarecrow Press, Inc.

Berkes, Ann. (2010 August 22) *Eternal Vigilance.* https://jeffersonlibrary.wordpress.com/2010/08/23/ eternal-vigilance/. (accessed 8-21-16)

Brueggemann, Walter, (1982) *Living Toward a Vision: Biblical Reflections on Shalom* Philadelphia, PA: United Church Press

Chicago Tribune (1986) *The American Millstone: An Examination of the Nation's Permanent Underclass* Chicago, IL: Contemporary Books

Eberstadt, Mary (1995 May 1) Putting Children Last. *Commentary Magazine.* Retrieved from https://www.commentarymagazine.com/articles/putting-children-last/

Hanlon, Mike, (2007 May 28) "World Population Becomes More Urban Than Rural," http://www.gizmag.com/go/7334 (accessed Aug 25, 2016)

Harvey, Paul and Goff, Phillip, editors, (2004) *The Columbia Documentary History of Religion in America Since 1945*, New York, NY: Columbia University Press, 287

Hillis, Dave, (2014) *Cities: Playgrounds or Battlegrounds—Leadership Foundations' Fifty Year Journey of Social and Spiritual Renewal.* Tacoma, Washington: Leadership Foundations Press

Hillis, Dave, Leadership Foundations Case Statement (March 2011)

http://www.abcdinstitute.org/ (accessed 8-21-16)

http://www.ccda.org/ (accessed 8-21-16)

http://www.rclinthicum.org/ (accessed 8-21-16)

https://appreciativeinquiry.case.edu/ (accessed 8-21-16)

Ingleton, Kieran, (2015 July 29) *The Evolution of the Polish Solidarity Movement.*
https://thevieweast.wordpress.com/2015/07/29/the-evolution-of-the-polish-solidarity-movement/ (accessed July 21, 2016)

IOM, (2011 July 19) *Population and Urbanization in Humanitarian Settings, ECOSOC Humanitarian Affairs Segment Side Event*, http://www.un.org/en/ecosoc/julyhls/pdf11/has_concept_note-population_and_urbanization_in_humanitarian_settings.pdf (accessed Aug 25, 2016)

John 1:14, The Message Bible

Jones, Jeffrey M., (2015 June 15) "Confidence in U.S. Institutions Still Below Historical Norms," Gallup, http://www.gallup.com/poll/183593/confidence-institutions-below-historical-norms.aspx (accessed Aug 25, 2016)

Langmead, Ross, (2004) *The Word Made Flesh: Towards an Incarnational Missiology.* Lanham, MD: University Press of America, Inc.

Leadership Foundations Case Statement, March 2011.

McKnight, John, (1995) *The Careless Society: Community and Its Counterfeits*. New York, NY: Basic Books, A Member of the Perseus Books Group

Over 200 million escape slums, (2010 March 18) *Over 200 million escape slums but overall number still rising, UN report finds*. http://www.un.org/apps/news/story.asp?NewsID=34119#.V6jI urgrKUk (accessed 8-8-2016)

Pearle, Lauren, (2016 February 12) "School Shootings Since Columbine: By the Numbers," ABC30, http://abcnews.go.com/US/school-shootings-columbine-numbers/story?id=36833245, (accessed July 28. 2016)

Pew Research Center, (2014 January 14) "Religious Hostilities Reach Six-Year High," Pew Research Center, http://www.pewforum.org/2014/01/14/religious-hostilities-reach-six-year-high/ (accessed Aug, 25, 2016)

Sheehan, Tim, (2015 October 17) Boxing Gym Will bring New Life to Old Fresno Warehouse," (October 17, 2015) The Fresno Bee. http://www.fresnobee.com/news/business/article39371634.htm l (accessed 8-20-16)

Shipley, David, (2012 November 14) *Making Sure Nonprofits Aren't All About Profit*. www.bloomberg.com/view/articles/2012-11-14/making-sure-nonprofits-aren-t-all-about-profit (accessed 8-8-16)

Stafford, Tim, (2000, March 6). Taking Fresno Back, *Christianity Today*, *Vol. 44*, (No. 3), 48

Stone, Trisi, Sherman and Hornton, (2016 July 29) "A Guide to Statistics on Historical Trends in Inequality," Center On Budget and Policy Priorities, http://www.cbpp.org/research/poverty-and-inequality/a-guide-to-statistics-on-historical-trends-in-income-inequality (Accessed July 31, 2016)

Tocqueville, Alexis de (1835) *Democracy in America*. London, England: Penguin Books

Truth and Reconciliation Commission Website, (n.d.) http://www.justice.gov.za/trc/

United Nations Human Settlements Programme. (2003) *The Challenge of Slums: Global Report on Human Settlements*

Watts, Jonathan, (2016 August 19) "Rio Police Killings of Favela Residents Continue as Games go on in Rio" The Guardian, https://www.theguardian.com/world/2016/aug/19/rio-police-killings-favela-residents-olympic-security-segregation (accessed 8-20-16)

Wolterstorff, Nicholas, (2004) *Educating for Shalom: Essays on Christian Higher Education* Grand Rapids, MI: William B. Eerdmans Publishing, 22-23.

Yoder, Perry (1997) *Shalom: The Bible's Word for Salvation, Justice, and Peace,* Nappanee IN: Evangel Publishing House, 5-6.

Chapter Two

Catalyzing Transformational City Movements

Randy White

FPU Center for Community Transformation

> *You can't steal second with your foot on first.*
>
> Fredrick Wilcox

If history turns on small hinges, can a shirtless guy doing a strange dance on a sunny hillside start a "movement?" Those of you who have seen Derek Sivers' three-minute YouTube video, *"Leadership Lessons from Dancing Guy,"* know it's possible. The small hinge is not the *lone nut*, as Sivers calls him, gyrating on the hill, flailing his arms in his eccentric dance at an outdoor picnic. No, the hinge is rather the first follower to join him. The *first follower* is encouraged by the lone nut, who is glad for the company and models the dance. But it is the first follower, the hinge, who motions to other friends—it's that guy who starts a movement. And then we see another join, which means, according to the narrator, "Three's a crowd and a crowd is news." Quickly we see others joining them, and they call to their friends. Eventually dozens stream down the hill to dance. Then comes the tipping point when hundreds of people covering the whole hillside join the dancing crowd, because to be left on the edges is now less desirable than being included in the strangeness. At the end of the video you can faintly hear someone say to a friend, "How did he do that? How did he do that?!"

What is a Movement?

You would be right, of course, if you said this wasn't a movement. It was an event—one that didn't last. The shirtless dancing guy had no objective other than to be exuberant. Followers are what created the "movement" as they motioned for people to join them, but there were no objectives beyond that. They didn't exist to accomplish anything. And yet the dynamics of real movements that we have seen in recent and not-so-recent history have had similar features.

Some are just as fleeting. We could cite the disorganized, here today-gone-tomorrow Occupy Wall Street movement. We could talk about Tiananmen Square that began with the idealism of college students and was crushed by the state. We could point to the early, inspiring days of the Arab Spring and the hope of democracy in the Middle East, which evaporated in the heat of chaos and power vacuums. All these were begun with the influence of key catalysts, their own versions of a lone nut, and the early adopters who fueled the momentum. But they all died, either violently or from the cancer of their own un-unified vision.

However, other movements faced the storms of opposition and the long slog of progress over time, and in their very longevity they fared differently from their flash-in-the-pan counterparts. They had intentional leadership, infrastructure, coherence, spiritual vision, broad participation, natural onramps to involvement, diverse jobs that got done, and clear outcomes in shaping both policy and social assumptions. One only has to think of Wilberforce and the Abolitionist Movement, Jane Addams and the broad-based Movement for Women's Suffrage, Martin Luther King, Jr. and the Civil Rights Movement, and Cesar Chavez' movement securing rights for farm workers. Though we have more to do in all these arenas, we are a different society today because of these movements.

This chapter is about igniting social change in the name of Jesus in ways that catalyze ongoing, sustainable spiritual and social transformation in cities. We will look at three main questions: What does it take to begin a transformational city movement? What does it take to mature and sustain a movement that transforms a city? And how do other factors like theology, leadership, and cross-city learning play into the process of starting and sustaining a transformational city movement?

To do this we will look inside a movement of city transformation that has been going on in Fresno for close to twenty-five years, seeing it through two helpful lenses: one from observers of social dynamics, and one from theologically motivated transformational leaders in a Christ-centered civic movement.

What Does It Take to Begin a Transformational City Movement?

In their work entitled *Making Change: How Social Movements Work and How to Support Them*, Manuel Pastor and Rhoda Ortiz from the University of Southern California identify 10 elements that successful social movements have in common:

1. A vision and frame
2. An authentic base
3. A commitment to the long haul
4. An underlying and viable economic model
5. A vision of government and governance
6. A scaffold of solid research
7. A pragmatic policy package
8. A recognition of the need for scale
9. A strategy for scaling up
10. A willingness to network with other movements

A history of how the movement for Fresno's transformation started was recounted in Chapter One. By reexamining the early days of Fresno's movement through the lens that Pastor and Ortiz have constructed, it's amazing to see how the Spirit of God took our leaders by the hand to put in place each of the ten elements.

First, "a vision and frame" were driven around the desperate demographics that gripped our city of 500,000, which found itself spiraling out of control in every social category in the early 1990s. There were 13,000 car thefts, 8,000 certified gang members, record murders (100 in 1993), low levels of educational attainment (60% graduation rate), concentrated poverty (the highest in the nation of all large cities (Brookings Institution Report, 2005) children living in poverty (nearly 4 of 10), and the distinction of being the meth capital of the U.S. We were sure of one thing: if we went on simply telling our anecdotal stories of how we were making a difference in our ministry silos, we would get more of what we had always gotten We were also sure that this was not acceptable, given the great challenges we were facing. More than an interest group or an issue, a passion for a transformed city became the "vision and frame" of our prayers, our gatherings, and our actions. The "vision and frame" were expressed in the mission statement of a multi-sector faith gathering we created called the "No Name Fellowship: Releasing God's Resources through Reconciled Relationships for the Rebuilding of Our City."

No Name Necessary to Catalyze Change

Next, "an authentic base" began to develop. Some initial infrastructure was created. We held monthly meetings to gather faith leaders from all the sectors—pastors, nonprofit leaders, elected and appointed officials, and business people.

Because this leadership group dubbed "No Name Fellowship" engaged the leaders of key institutions critical to the welfare of the city in a spirit of support and service, there developed a liturgy of sorts based on Three E's developed with the help of urbanologist Dr. Jim Westgate: to EXPOSE them to a current challenge in the city (violence, refugees, hunger, educational crisis, unemployment, and others), then to EXCHANGE the latest best practices in dealing with those challenges, and then to mobilize some form of EMBRACE of that challenge by people of faith. We were inadvertently developing "a scaffold of solid research" and "a pragmatic policy package" primarily out of our commitment to serve those institutional experts in law enforcement, education, health care, business, probation, and other areas key to the health of our city. And because of the early commitment to be a group of multi-sector leaders, there has been, for the most part, a built-in "willingness to network with other movements," another key element.

From the beginning, leaders made "a commitment to the long haul." Someone suggested we incorporate as a nonprofit 501(c)(3). But as mentioned in chapter one, in a crucial moment, we all remembered a wise and experienced leader said, "No, let's not do that. If we give ourselves a name we will think we're doing something, and the situation is so desperate, we can't afford to think that." This, of course, turned into the "No Name Fellowship," which has now continued as an organism rather than an organization for more than two decades, again building "an authentic base." Now No Name is an organic piece of key infrastructure designed to create onramps for people of faith to embrace their city. It operates with a volunteer steering committee, with no funding, and with no guarantees of a future.

In retrospect, what emerged had been an "underlying and viable economic model" based primarily on building faith-based, grass-roots, church-supported organizations, networks, and events that fed a very alive movement for transformation in our city. Now one could ask, "Is dependence on faith-based or church funding really a viable economic model?" In 1995 a group of us met with Peter Drucker, arguably the foremost business consultant of the 20th Century, who made a statement that both confirmed and challenged our thinking. Drucker stated that "the Church is the only institution capable of recivilizing broken urban environments." When asked what was the basis for and the data behind this bold assertion, Drucker simply stated that the Church generates more hours of volunteer involvement and more money in community investment than any other institution in a city. True to Drucker's claim, the Church in Fresno, taken as a whole, has been the economic engine standing behind the many expressions of Christ Centered Civic Transformation that have emerged over the last decade and a half. While other sources of economic support have emerged, the Church remains the pivotal resource.

From the beginning, because of the huge, citywide challenges and the multi-sector leaders that drove the movement, there was "a recognition of the need for scale" and a "strategy for scaling up" that has expressed itself over the last 25 years as this fledgling transformational city movement has matured. We will look at this scaling up process below. But all in all, every one of the 10 elements critical to successful social movements identified by Pastor and Ortiz were embedded in the early years of the No Name Fellowship.

What Does It Take to Mature and Sustain a Movement that Transforms a City?

What are we to make of this all-too-rare landscape that has emerged in Fresno? What could be learned about movement making for other cities? There have been some signs along the way that what started as a desperation-driven, spontaneous, "Dancing Guy with a First Follower or Two" movement has over time matured into something more sustainable. For instance, when Billy Graham did one of his last two crusades in Fresno in 2001 right after 9/11 and after his organization spent a year here working with local leaders to set it up, he remarked to several of us, "I think Fresno may be the most connected city in America."

In retrospect, what we experienced then and what continues today is what Tim Keller, Pastor of Redeemer Church in New York City, refers to as a "gospel movement." Keller cites what he believes is the unifying factor inherent to movements—the alignment of personal preference (Keller, 2012, 339). It is a group of people who want the same thing or something similar, who have a sense of the future that they prefer and are willing to work toward. Malcomb Gladwell called this the *Law of the Few*—a key ingredient in what we want to become a *social epidemic* (Gladwell, 2002, 33).

Movement Theology

Pastor and Ortiz provide one lens to interpret how Fresno experienced the beginnings of a genuine social movement, and Keller's Gospel movement, which we will return to examine in greater depth in a moment, provides another lens. But is there such a thing as "a theology of movement" that fuels the development of transformational city movements and compels people to join? We want to briefly explore this first, as theological vision provides the foundation for this transformational movement. This movement theology might include a tri-focal lens, so to speak: a theology of *Ingress and Egress*, a theology of *Infection,* and a theology of *Identity.*

By *theology of Ingress and Egress* we mean how God has moved people groups, often in response to their cries, in the accomplishment of God's will. The shalom community is certainly what God wanted for his people in Egypt. But after generations in slavery there, it was clearly not possible. In Exodus 3 the cries of his people move God to action, and God calls the people out:

> Then the Lord said, "I have observed the misery of my people who are in Egypt; I have heard their cry on account of their taskmasters. Indeed, I know their sufferings, and I have come down to deliver them from the Egyptians, and to bring them up out of that land to a good and broad land, a land flowing with milk and honey, to the country of the Canaanites, the Hittites, the Amorites, the Perizzites, the Hivites, and the Jebusites. The cry of the Israelites has now come to me; I have also seen how the Egyptians oppress them. (Exod 3:7–9).

Thus, in compassionate response to the cry of suffering, through a primarily political process, God initiates an *egress* of God's people from that place, their literal mass *removal* (or movement), a physical, geographic movement that ultimately positioned them to function as a theocratic movement following the covenant at Sinai (Exod 24)—an identity moving toward a purpose. What emerges over the next generation is the refining of that movement during the wilderness years and eventually the *ingress* of God's people to the Promised Land (the ultimate symbol of shalom's promised abundance and plenty), where they are to live out the identity God has given them. It is that period of wandering that has come to symbolize the transformational process necessary in leaders, in groups, in social systems, and in a sense of destination and purpose necessary to achieve shalom. Perhaps this God-initiated process of *egress* and *ingress* is a precursor to what the Apostle Paul would refer to as he spoke to the Athenian elite on the Aereopagus when in Acts 17:26–27 he said,

From one ancestor he made all nations to inhabit the whole
earth, and he allotted the times of their existence and the
boundaries of the places where they would live, so that they
would search for God and perhaps grope for him and find him—
though indeed he is not far from each one of us.

The hand of God has something to do with where people live. If
this is true then it is also true when those places change, when there are
mass movements out of and into a place. We are seeing changes of this
sort all over the world as natural disaster and war put people on the move
in the form of refugee movements, as climate change begins to erase
island nations, as economic migrants seek a better life. The cries of
people in those often vulnerable circumstances reach the ears of God.
This passage suggests there is something about the physical place, the
habitations of people, and about changes in that habitation that influence
our human search for God. Perhaps we instinctively know that God is
listening to our cries. It is a cry to let us emerge from what enslaves us,
from what limits us, from what devalues us, from what erodes our
dignity, from being mere pawns in the cold schemes of others. So it is a
cry for *egress*. And it is a cry for *ingress*, a longing to be called toward
something, called into something beautiful.

It was the cry of those journeying the Underground Railroad
movement, *egress* from the slavery of the south, *ingress* to the freedom
of the north. Today it is the cry of the Black Lives Matter movement,
egress from racially biased policy and an unequal justice system, *ingress*
toward respect and equal protection under the law.

In our city, this theology causes us to see migration patterns in a
new light. Economic migrants from Mexico and Central America who
seek work, as well as their counterparts from other parts of our own State
seeking more modest housing prices, move here giving thanks to God for
a city where they find blessing and together become parts of our new

reality. Egress and ingress under the sovereignty of God, a new creation in the making.

Infection. The people of God in exile, Israel, had to figure out how to retain their identity as a Yahweh-worshipping people after being ripped out of their homeland. We can imagine just how remarkably hard this was as they sat by the river en-route to Babylon and openly confessed not knowing how they could "sing the Lord's song in a foreign land" (Ps 137). Most of them were hoping this was going to be short-lived and they would soon be going home. But Jeremiah's letter confirmed their worst nightmare—that they would be in Babylon for a generation. They had been victims of a cruel siege, and now were to serve a foreign power against their will. But God didn't see it that way. As God makes clear through Jeremiah, his strategy is to plant them as a shalom pathogen, a spiritual Trojan horse, in the heart of the most evil city on the planet. This was God asking them to adopt a *Theology of Infection.* They are to settle in, plant gardens, build houses, marry off their children, and seek the well-being, the prosperity, the security, the peace, the flourishing of that city (Jer 29:4–7). Their own flourishing, he promised, would be bound up in being that kind of movement. And to seal the emotional part of that commitment, they were even to pray for it. We don't know if the people of Israel saw the brilliance of the strategy. As captives, it would take a lot to have your vision of yourself transformed from *victim* into *movement* of the Most High God. But if in their vulnerable state they listened to the prophet and his letter from God, this would have been a recipe for transformation, the simultaneous commitment of thousands of people for the transformation of a place God cared about. We call that a movement. In our city, this has taken the shape of a significant relocation movement, or *strategic neighboring,* at first instigated by Baby Boomer generation leaders who took the plunge into our most neglected neighborhoods and who then told the stories that emerged from the experience. These stories took hold in the imagination of Gen X and Millennial leaders who joined the growing movement.

Along with a theology that sees God's movement of people in response to their cries and a theology that sees the infectious nature of God's call upon a people, a theology of *Identity* also provides fuel for transformational city movements. It is noted in the biblical record (Acts 11:26) that the followers of Jesus were first called Christians in the city of Antioch, which was the capital of the Roman province of Syria (New Bible Dictionary, 1962, 51). It was an amazingly diverse place, a significant center with stunning temples, architectural wonders, a vibrant commercial and entertainment center, and inhabitants that had gained a "reputation for energy, insolence and instability" (NBD, 1962, 51). Why was it there that followers of Jesus were given (perhaps pejoratively) the nickname *Christians* or *Christ ones*, or *little Christs*? What characteristics had they taken on that gave them an identity as a group in the imaginations of the inhabitants? I think there are several. We know that Nicolas was one of the seven deacons of Acts 6:5 and was from Antioch. Did he come back home and continue the practice of equal care for the widows in the newly planted Antioch Church, the first of its kind? Did the elders of that church, many of whom were refugees (Acts 11:20) from the persecution following the stoning of Stephen, demonstrate an egalitarian, cross-cultural approach to ministry that became visible to the residents? Did news of Paul's confrontation of Peter regarding his hypocrisy of not eating with Gentiles, when VIP leaders were visiting from the Jewish church in Jerusalem (Gal 2) get out and become part of how the church was seen—as a place where these ethnic barriers were being broken down? Did the fact that its pastoral leadership team included two men from Africa, one from the Mediterranean, one from

Asia Minor, and one from the Middle East, (Acts 4:36; 9:11; 13:1), provide the church with a "visible witness and a model of unity at the highest level"? (DeYmaz and Li, 2010, 42.) Did the fact that Paul began and ended his second missionary journey there suggest to Antiochans that this was indeed more than an isolated group, but something with radically different sociological intentions and norms, something that had structure and a particular goal, something that had the fragrance of a quality of life that was attractive and different—something we might call a transformational movement? In our city this sense of identity and mission has become an important alternative to the negative self-image so many suffer from here. It is one that rejects the easy cowardice of cynicism, and embraces the African cry of *Harambee*—"let's get together and push!"

And even as God moves or allows movement of whole people groups, as God moves them with purpose to influence and shape, God moves the psychology of a people to see itself differently. In our city this has meant movement to a new mindset, one which for the longest time in our low self-esteem has been hard to believe really existed or is possible. This new space is characterized by attitudes of abundance rather than deficit; it cherishes our assets and does not get paralyzed by our needs. It is one which, in the vision of Zechariah 8, asks us to imagine a city where the most vulnerable, the elderly with their canes, and the children in their defenselessness, are safe and secure and provided for in the shalom city. When cities create an environment of shalom (of peace, abundance, reconciliation) for even the most vulnerable members, they have become the beloved community. Our city has begun to believe that this is possible, that this is our *identity*, even as reality says we are still a long way off.

Ministry Ecosystem

So now back to Keller. Pastor/Theologian Tim Keller provides an additional lens for us in his concept of a ministry ecosystem, in his book *Center Church*, this fertile, interdependent network of vision-driven relationships has been developing in Fresno for twenty-five years. A ministry ecosystem is where collaboration around key components and strategies built on a contextualized theological vision becomes a normative way of supporting a healthy and fertile environment. Keller describes four key components and six strategies characteristic of a maturing movement with a thriving ministry ecosystem, and we will look at Fresno's story through these lenses:

Four Key Components (Keller, 2012, 375)

Compelling vision

Culture of sacrificial commitment and intrinsic reward

Generous flexibility toward other organizations

Spontaneous birth of new ideas and leaders and growth from within

Six Strategies

Citywide Prayer

Specialist evangelism

Justice and mercy ministries

Vocational/faith initiatives

Institutions of theological training

Leaders who come together

Looking at Fresno's ongoing movement development through the lens of Keller's Four Key Components helps see how a ministry ecosystem is formed and how it works on the ground.

Four Components of a Ministry Ecosystem

1. Compelling Vision

First, Keller, like Pastor and Ortiz, says there must be a compelling vision. The vision behind Fresno's movement has continued to center around the transformation of the city, whether expressed by No Name's catch phrase "rebuilding our city," or one Mayor's call to see Fresno move from being "A Tale of Two Cities to the Story of One Community," or Fresno Pacific University's establishment of the "Center for Community Transformation." Leaders began to pull foundational concepts from Scripture that inform the phenomenon of transformational movements. The etymology of the word "transformation" is instructive. *Trans* refers to movement (as in *trans*portation) and *form* refers to a structure or shape or system. The Greek equivalent is *metamorphosis*, referring to the kind of *trans*ition to a new form that happens in the development of a chrysalis into a butterfly. So what is the new form that we have been creating a movement toward in our city? Over time it became abundantly clear that we were all talking about the Bible's "shalom community" characterized by justice, righteousness, and peace.

In our city the vision behind our transformational movement is intentionally undergirded by a theology of shalom—making things the way they should be (Yoder, 1987, 12). There are core texts that older leaders have kept in front of younger leaders that describe the goal of the new community including Isaiah 65 with its "new heavens and the new earth," Zechariah 8 with its old and young alike thriving in the new city, and Martin Luther King's *Beloved Community*. The "how" of transformation has also been built on a biblical vision leaning on sources like Jeremiah 29:4–7 and the call to "seek the peace of the city," or John Perkins' "Three Rs: Relocation, Reconciliation, Redistribution" of Christian Community Development. This vision, compellingly communicated, is what helps individual preferences—or the longings that people have for their city—take shape and get unified, and it's what attracts young leaders to link their lives and become involved in achieving it. This compelling vision of making our city an inspiration has also begun to heal the low-grade depression bordering on self-loathing that Fresnans have internalized with years of daily news stories reminding them of negative social indicators, and "Fresno jokes" on late night television shows. The compelling vision of transformation based on shalom inspires us to become more than we are.

2. Culture of sacrificial commitment and intrinsic reward

Keller maintains that a compelling vision leads to *A culture of sacrificial commitment and intrinsic reward* (Keller, 2012, 339). In other words, leaders model sacrificial commitment for no other reward than the knowledge that they are responding to a work of God, and others follow that lead. In our city this took the shape of a relocation movement with key leaders moving from the safest neighborhoods of the suburbs to the highest-crime, highest-poverty neighborhood of the city, one that was being called "The Devil's Triangle" at the time for its gangs, drugs, and poverty. This created splash in the city and led to the spotlight being placed on the stories of suffering being experienced in that previously-ignored neighborhood, as well as the resilience and strength of many residents who had called Lowell home for generations. As the movement toward relocation began to grow with the addition of mechanisms to connect young leaders to neighborhoods like the Devil's

Triangle, other forms of sacrificial commitment and intrinsic reward grew. For instance, there was a growing sense in the leadership community that those who were taking the issues and challenges of the city seriously were developing new levels of camaraderie with colleagues, fresh initiatives to align ministries around, and the strangeness—dare we recognize it?—of the presence of *hope* that no one had felt in a long time. Intrinsic reward, indeed.

3. Generous flexibility toward other organizations

To Keller a *generous flexibility toward other organizations* means "cooperating with anyone who shares an interest in the vision" (Keller, 2012, 340). Movements may have institutional stewards, but in our experience institutions are not movement marionettes—they do not hold the strings. In a ministry ecosystem such as ours many institutions, from churches to nonprofits, each place their shoulders to the big rock we are trying to move. One of the pieces of spiritual infrastructure leaders created here was a monthly gathering of faith-based nonprofits called City Builders Round Table, hosted by Evangelicals for Social Action, a Community Benefit Organization (CBO) that specializes in city-wide relief ministry which mobilizes churches and other CBOs. At these gatherings CBOs do cooperative training, share resources, and have even attempted joint fundraising. As a result, such a level of commitment has been cultivated that when one agency was threatened with the loss of funding from the city, another willingly removed itself from the funding pipeline to preserve funds for their sister organization.

4. Spontaneous birth of new ideas and leaders and growth from within

Keller's description of "spontaneous birth of new ideas and leaders and growth from within" (Keller, 2012, 340) fits Fresno's movement culture that has been crafted over the last two decades. There is an organic nature of this movement because it is not being directed by a single entity, yet it impacts the entire city. This creates a fertile environment for innovation, as well as an exponential form of growth as there are no bottlenecks to leadership. In a culture where transformation is the North Star that key institutions and leaders are pointing to, it turns out there are a thousand onramps to becoming part of the movement.

For example, InterVarsity, a campus ministry, began urban service and learning projects, placing college students in high crime, high poverty neighborhoods to work alongside urban ministers in bringing change. That ministry became an onramp for young emerging leaders to find their place in the city, creating structures as simple as a tutoring program and as complex as a residential urban ministry training house (The Pink House) where emerging leader residents spent a year learning about leadership, biblical community, and urban ministry. This led to a multiplication of urban, residential ministry training centers or houses in the city dedicated to developing leaders focused on transformation. Some are church-based and others recruit nationally. They have now formed an Association of Ministry Houses training dozens of emerging leaders annually. This has fueled a relocation movement in the city, channeling a steady stream of leaders to settle in and make a life in the highest-poverty neighborhoods, transformed to be agents of transformation.

Another example, *Hope Now for Youth,* grew out of this phenomenon. At one of the early stages in the movement pastors and leaders in the city gathered for citywide prayer, the first strategy of Keller's ministry ecosystem. This meeting happened at the same time as the riots that broke out in Los Angeles following the beating of Rodney King. As LA burned, and as one of the pastors drove home from this meeting, he began to weep. Roger Minassian was in a comfortable position as senior pastor, within a few years of retirement. By his own description he is a fairly stoic man, saying, "Up until this point I had only cried one other time in my life, when my mother had died." What had made this pastor weep was the emergence of a question he could not answer. "What would cause a people to be so full of despair that they would burn their *own* neighborhoods down?" he asked himself, bewildered. He returned home and began to sense a call to begin a ministry for gang members, to get them job ready and place them in full-time positions. This was, of course, ridiculous since he had never met a gang member. But now, 20 years later, they have placed their 2,000th former gang member in a full-time job.

A final example is Artie Padilla, who had a vision for linking churches to the challenged educational system in the city which graduated barely half of its students. In just 10 years, with the encouragement of a healthy transformational movement, *Every Neighborhood Partnership* has now matched churches to fifty of the ninety elementary schools in the city. These churches provide afterschool programs, Saturday sports clubs, in-class reading assistance, and even campus improvement projects for the schools. And in every classroom that has been matched with the church, benchmarking is done and scores have improved. This has made the Church the largest ally of the city's educational systems. These strategies could not have succeeded or been sustained without the ministry ecosystem we worked together to cultivate and the transformational movement that has been birthed as a result.

A word of caution is appropriate here. Even as our movement has grown to experience the "spontaneous birth of new ideas and leaders and growth from within" that Keller describes, this has meant the death of other structures, groups, and organizations. The formation of No Name Fellowship and the exciting spin-off meetings and gatherings drew time and attention from other long-standing groups that had met for years and which simply went away. And, as the organic No Name phenomenon experienced some early wins, it became clear that an organizational structure was needed to sustain some of the initiatives being generated. A local leadership foundation, modeled after the Pittsburgh Leadership Foundation, was established and functioned for ten years. But with the 2008 recession, the leadership foundation that had played such a crucial role in the early years of the movement had several leadership transitions, then funding challenges, and eventually closed. This organization that had played an instrumental role in the birth of Pastors Clusters, The No-Name Fellowship, mentoring programs for the children of prisoners, tutoring programs and reading clubs, public-private partnerships for city projects, and a host of other initiatives that helped to set a tone in the city that made faith-based civic engagement normative was suddenly gone.

At first, we all held our collective breath, wondering what would happen to these initiatives. But over the next several years it became clear that these programs, and especially the values that undergirded them, had been embedded successfully in the imaginations of faith leaders. In some instances other nonprofit agencies picked up the programs and became the new stewards. In other cases programs spun off and became their own ministries, supported by a strong ministry ecosystem. The point is that ministry ecosystems experience death as well as birth in an ongoing set of changes that result from pursuing the overall transformation of a city.

And it's happening again. At this writing we are seeing the beginning of the end for another key organization that birthed many of the initial onramps that young emerging leaders have come to rely on. These included accessible chances for college-age leaders to dip their toe in urban and service learning projects, chances to develop relationships with inner-city kids through tutoring, chances to study the macro issues facing our city, chances to live for a year in a residential urban ministry training center and intern at a local nonprofit. This institution has for 25 years provided these opportunities and onramps. And although it is hard to imagine our city without them, the challenges of staffing, of leadership turnover, of the parent organizations readjusting priorities over time, and uncertainties in funding can erode even the best of organizations. Stakeholders in our city transformation movement are now gathering with the director to talk about options for carrying on the most important aspects of what they do to feed the movement and to provide those pathways for involvement if they close. And we are praying that this crisis becomes an opportunity for a new host to steward those key pathways in a fresh way. That's what movements that have become ministry ecosystems do.

6 Strategies of a Ministry Ecosystem

According to Keller, just as there are Four Key Components to a healthy ministry ecosystem, there are six strategies that characterize a maturing movement. These also provide a helpful perspective to see the inner workings of a city's transformational work. I hope that looking at Fresno's 25 year-old city transformation movement through the lens of Keller's Six Strategies will spark your imagination for opportunities in your own city:

Strategy #1: Citywide Prayer

Seeing prayer as strategic has been a hallmark of Fresno's transformational city movement. Along with a historic, desperate, multi-cultural and multi-denominational four-day prayer gathering that many look to as the beginning of the movement in the early 1990s, there has been a consistent, intentional, mostly coordinated commitment to ongoing prayer. This includes weekly men's and women's prayer gatherings in churches, more and more inclusive of citywide concerns; weekly pastors prayer gatherings; citywide and regional pastors and ministry leaders prayer retreats; and an annual citywide prayer breakfast of 1000-2000 participants. Significant resources are provided by individual leaders and key organizations to give leadership and structure to these prayer initiatives. All of this is punctuated by special vigils, prayer gatherings, and ceremonies prompted by times of distress like an act of senseless violence; the launch of a new ministry or initiative; or times of difficulty, like we are experiencing now with persistent lack of rainfall and drought. Reference is regularly made to the invisible intercessors such as our communities of retired nuns whose prayers mysteriously but powerfully engage the Spirit to shape and move the principalities and powers in heavenly places on behalf of our city. It is often said that prayer is the "air war" going before and standing behind the "ground game" of Christ-centered civic transformation in Fresno.

Strategy #2: Specialist evangelism

One of the understandings that comes from a theological commitment to shalom is a comprehensive view of the peace of our city that makes an intrinsic, holistic, and unrelenting connection between personal transformation—the changed life of an individual—with the social transformation we seek for our city.

At the same time, it has taken wisdom and the development of social capital with key institutional leaders, like those in education and law enforcement as well as leaders of other faith communities and traditions, to navigate a pathway to ministry that avoids merely using social engagement around felt needs as an automatic doorway to Gospel proclamation without regard for the freedom, customs, values, beliefs, or culture of others.

Here are some lessons learned in fulfilling the call to communicate the life-changing message of Jesus Christ while engaging the multi-cultural, multi-sector reality of our American City:

- Develop and maintain strong capacity for specialist evangelism in the private spaces of your city. The fact that we have churches and Christian organizations like Christian Business Men's and Women's Connection in our city, skilled in and dedicated to communicating the Gospel in ways that allow people to make a life-changing decision for Christ, is Crucial to the vitality of a city. This means there are multiple places where individuals can voluntarily and by invitation hear and engage the Gospel.

- Resist proselytization, defined as when we use public spaces or resources to communicate religious messages in ways that are perceived as coercive or non-voluntary.

- Know the rules. Public spaces can become private spaces, as when a group of Christian students (not teachers or outside adults) under the "Equal Access" laws, use school facilities during lunch or before or after school for religious gatherings. Or when chaplains, under the auspices of a law enforcement agency, allow inmates to voluntarily access activities sponsored by religious groups of all persuasions in a correctional facility. Nothing can set a Gospel movement back faster than when willful or disrespectful church folk enter the public space with a sense of religious entitlement.

· Earn the right to be heard. When people of faith join with people of good will to serve the critical issues facing a city, the Spirit creates room for evangelism. There is nothing more sacred than when a city leader, having come to trust faith leaders serving her at a time when her institution was in crisis, has a private conversation that leads privately to radical life change.

There is now a new and exciting form of specialized evangelism emerging in Fresno, a church planting movement in the city designed to plant and grow churches strategically in Fresno's 22 poorest neighborhoods. They especially appeal to people wanting to go beyond attractional church models, instead preferring to create onramps for worship with varied and joyful acts of community engagement. Personal and social transformation are clapping hands together in celebration.

Strategy #3: Justice and mercy ministries

Maturing city movements have the capacity to respond to clear crises in human need and address the underlying justice issues involved. For instance, what can be done about the alarming increase in human trafficking? When three Christian women asked that question in our city, they each responded by focusing their expertise on creative angles addressing anti-human trafficking efforts. Andrea Shabaglian created a fashion line that raises money for International Justice Mission's human trafficking work and serves survivors. Jessica Pittman founded Central Valley Justice Coalition to raise awareness and mobilize the church. Melissa Gomez took on the reigns of the Freedom Coalition sponsored by the Economic Opportunities Commission which does prevention and education.

Similarly creative responses are taking place in the area of helping school children traumatized by family and neighborhood violence develop resiliency, a new initiative of our Police chaplaincy. Latino and non-immigrant pastors have mobilized with a number of ministries, local law enforcement, and ag-business leaders to address comprehensive immigration reform. They have formed the 3B's coalition—Bibles, Badges, and Business—to join the national movement to encourage federal action in addressing our broken immigration system.

In view of national concerns around race, police shootings, the Ferguson riots, and the voices in the Black Lives Matter movement, local clergy groups, the No Name Fellowship, and Faith in Fresno, a faith-based community organizing network, have been convening various conversations and action groups around issues related to race, building the capacity of our citizens and faith leaders to prevent and proactively address issues that arise in our own city. Community policing and the role of an independent police auditor are just a couple of the public policy issues that are being informed by these actions.

Transformational movements catalyze talent and coordinate it around the ever-evolving justice and mercy issues facing our cities.

Strategy #4: Vocational/faith initiatives

Addressing issues of jobs and vocation involves a maturity in city movements that connects both marketplace leaders and their workplaces and those needing to be engaged in the economic mainstream of the city. We have mentioned Hope Now for Youth, a ministry mentoring gang members and finding them jobs that has now placed their two-thousandth former gang member in a full-time job. But a request from our Mayor a few years ago required an even deeper, more systemic form of engagement connecting jobs, the church, and the economy through a vocational/faith initiative.

Faith-Rooted Social Enterprise and Entrepreneurship

In our city, concentrated poverty has been the norm for so many generations it has become obvious that no amount of charity, no multiplication of church programs that feed or clothe the poor, will ever suffice. And so a new initiative for faith-rooted social enterprise has begun to take hold. Leaders are hoping it becomes yet another on-ramp toward transformation, yet another stream in this growing movement to see our city reflect the shalom of God. As in all initiatives it had an initial catalyst. The mayor of Fresno at the time, Ashley Swearengin, came to several of us in the faith community, and being a serious follower of Christ herself, asked us to consider how the resources of Fresno's broad faith community could be brought to the table in addressing our defining challenge: unemployment that routinely surpassed three times the national average. Several of us undertook a year-long task of researching what churches and nonprofits across the country had successfully done to address unemployment, especially for people who had barriers to employment such as having been formerly incarcerated or having low levels of employable skills. What we found at times amazed us and simultaneously encouraged us because of the modesty of the models we were seeing. Even the smallest churches had found approaches to starting small businesses that had a social impact in mind and were self-sustaining financially. These most often reflected a small-is-beautiful approach, with each church or faith-based nonprofit employing just a handful of people. There was the small, African-American church in Albany, Georgia where the pastor had met six men in prison who had come to Christ and turned their lives around. They all got out of prison about the same time and of course came to the pastor for help. But even with his great reference, none of them were able to find employment after having to check the box on every application that asked about their criminal record. Pastor Greg lost patience with the system that was stacked against these men and decided that the church would start a small party rental supply business called "Just Jump Rentals." They would rent bounce houses. This provided some structure for these men, a chance to learn employable skills, and—even though it was just part time—some much-needed income. This worked so well that Pastor Greg started the second business at the church, *Agape Movers*. That business worked so well it was eventually picked up by U-Haul as a subsidiary. The men had jobs and new lives, the church grew, the Gospel advanced. Win, win, win. Then there was the church in Vancouver, British Columbia that started three small businesses: A catering company employing women recently released from prison (Just Catering), a renovation company employing men coming out of addictions (Just Renos), and a pottery studio (Just Pottery) employing developmentally disabled adults. Each of these businesses accomplished a social good while being self-sustaining.

Our research team published these stories and dozens more in a book called *The Work of Our Hands: Faith Rooted Approaches to Job Creation, Job Training, or Job Placement in a Context of Concentrated Poverty* (Condeopress.com, 2012). We then gave this book to 75% of all churches in Fresno, all faith-based nonprofits, 400 businesspeople, and the Mayor and City Council members. This had the impact of validating the category of social enterprise as a legitimate form of ministry and a viable strategy for poverty alleviation. But after this accomplishment we began to sense that more was required. If we had hoped to stimulate a movement of faith-rooted social enterprise, we would have to invest more in the model.

The Center for Community Transformation (CCT) at Fresno Pacific Biblical Seminary, acting as an institutional backbone for this aspect of the movement, began a series of summits on social enterprise. We hoped a modest 40 or 50 leaders would show up for the first summit, since it was such an out-of-the-box subject. But more than 120 came. The next year it was 140. The next year 175, and the momentum builds. The speakers and workshops all focused on why and how faith-based institutions are good hosts for social businesses. We laid both theological and pragmatic foundations, and we invited businesspeople to bring their skill sets to the table.

At the same time as these growing summits, the CCT raised money for a pitch-fest competition for social enterprise ideas that we called the Spark Tank. In the first year we raised a mere $7,500 and awarded three proposals put forward by churches and nonprofits for social enterprise models. We call these investments, not grants. One church designed a street level ad design and distribution model, Say Hello Advertising, that can saturate a business district with fliers, employing indigenous members of an inner-city neighborhood who hand-deliver them for less than the price of bulk mail. A nonprofit designed an inner-city fitness club called 701 United for kids in the highest crime zip code, each of whom pay $15 per month to learn martial arts and get in shape. But they are simultaneously taught conflict mediation and Christian discipleship. They are mentored and poured into by caring staff.

In the second year we raised double the amount ($15,000) and awarded seven proposals, including a cleaning service at a local women's shelter (Five Gals Cleaning), a translation services business at the local refugee ministry (FIRM Translation), a water-wise landscaping company at a local church (RockPile Yard Service) employing formerly incarcerated men, and a café at a local nonprofit employing fatherless young men (YMI Café).

In the third year we raised $26,000 and awarded 10 proposals, including a café to employ people coming out of the rescue mission program (Tree of Life Café). Ten additional start-up were awarded investments in this year's Spark Tank.

In each of these cases, we sent staff from each church or nonprofit to a series of business classes offered by the Small Business Administration, as well as assigned MBA students from the University to walk alongside them and accomplish small projects to help them get off the ground. We also made mentors available to them. As a backbone organization to this part of the transformational movement in our city, these are the small facilitations and encouragements necessary to turn the flicker into a full flame. It's too early to tell whether this will generate its own momentum beyond what we as an institution orchestrate. The escalating amounts of money being raised, the increased numbers of every summit, the clear growth in the number of proposals being submitted every year all suggest that this has the potential for becoming a strong stream in support of the transformation of our Valley. Only time will tell.

Strategy #5: Institutions of Theological Training

One mark of movement maturity is when what began with grass roots personal action spurs organized responses in terms of new ministries that are then embraced by local institutions of theological training. As the movement of Christ-centered Civic Transformation has grown in Fresno, so has its embrace by Fresno Pacific University's Biblical Seminary.

From the beginning, FPU's president was involved on the board of the No Name Fellowship and then the Fresno Leadership Foundation. Later, the seminary began to offer courses in Christian Community Development and today offers a Master's Degree in Community Leadership and Transformation.

But perhaps the most significant step on the part of the Seminary has been establishing the Center for Community Transformation (CCT), an institution within its own institution designed to build the movement of civic transformation in Fresno and in our Central California Region.

CCT's vision is to see "equal access to all the blessings of our region—an abundant community that flourishes with entrepreneurial creativity, spiritual freedom, economic vitality and justice, environmental integrity, cross cultural/social collaboration and political health." Its mission is "to provide a faith-rooted, institutional engine and catalyst for systemic and sustainable transformation into a unique region of communities characterized by abundance and peace."

It carries out its mission through initiatives in the areas of research, convening, and training. Initiatives include faith-based job creation and social enterprise, financial literacy in extreme poverty neighborhoods, a certificate program in pastoral and ministry leadership for Latino pastors, and various civic renewal efforts in areas ranging from civic leadership development to anti-trafficking efforts to comprehensive immigration reform and adult education and literacy. The CCT basic question is always, "How might God's people be equipped to serve and shape the systems of the city for the common good?"

Strategy #6: Leaders Who Come Together

Keller's sixth strategy that characterizes a maturing ministry ecosystem is a city's capacity to gather its leaders. Here are four interesting ways Fresno has seen leaders come together:

Gathering Leaders in Community

For the last twenty years, some of the more than forty leaders who have relocated intentionally to the Lowell Neighborhood in Central Fresno in order to seek its peace have met every Sunday night to pray together and to share both the tribulations of living in a high crime neighborhood and the small victories that play out every day. We eat together and remind ourselves of the values that keep us here and that frame the way we spend our days. We plan neighborhood outreaches together, we tell stories, and on many occasions we have found ourselves knit together in tears. All of this provides encouragement to the heart of the movement.

Gathering Pastor Leaders for Fellowship and Community Betterment

At a certain point in the development of the city movement in Fresno, two things were clear: leadership would have to include more pastors and the leadership structure would have to stretch beyond the No Name Fellowship. At this point, Gordon Donoho, a former pastor who had become a key leader in various citywide leadership organizations, was tasked with addressing this issue. In meeting with pastors, Gordon began gathering pastors in geocentric clusters, now called Pastors' Clusters. There are now thirteen of these clusters that meet monthly and are involving about a third of all churches in the city to build relationships around the goal of neighborhood transformation. Pastor Eli Loera now leads a steering committee made up of pastors from each group, stewarding a process that has kept the attention of the clusters on their neighborhoods.

Gathering Pastors and Leaders Around Issues of Social Justice and Equity

Across the country, most local efforts to give voice to disenfranchised communities around issues of justice and equity are based on organizing clergy and their congregations. This is also true in Fresno where Faith in Fresno, a PICO affiliate, was organized for this specific purpose. Over the last several years, FIF has helped Fresno address issues of race, payday lending, the lack of public infrastructure such as parks, and a city general plan that reprioritized a portion of the city's resources for the rebuilding of downtown inner core neighborhoods.

Gathering Young Leaders by Providing Onramps for Engagement

One of the most exciting leadership success stories in Fresno has been the creation of pathways that have gathered and engaged emerging leaders. Some of these pathways have been short-term immersion experiences and study opportunities that have provided long and gentle introductions to city life, to poverty, and to injustice and may include volunteering at a tutoring program or fixing a broken porch in a neglected neighborhood, while leaders help to debrief, interpret, and reflect on what's happening there. Others provide a little steeper and shorter onramp, and include living in a ministry house (like those mentioned earlier) in an urban neighborhood and serving a local agency in an internship, while engaging in deep conversation around urban sociology and theology. And still others offer even steeper onramps including involvement at a policy level on a contentious issue by walking publicly alongside neighborhoods confronting unjust city systems. The work has been the intentional construction of progressive levels of onramp with ever-escalating steps in city transformational activity. The gift has been the successive waves of capable leaders who, having discovered their leadership, are now fully engaged in our city, exercising sustainable influence.

And that movement now nurtures a larger city transformation process that at this writing reaches over 400 leaders in the 20-30 age group every year in a Christian Community Development training event called Fresno City Summit. Amazingly, this annual process is led by a coalition of individual and institutional volunteers who plan, fundraise, recruit for, and staff the event. Fresno City Summit connects emerging leaders to transformational ministry agents and opportunities throughout the city, as well as to each other.

Twenty-five years ago, Fresno was in crisis. By looking at how leaders of faith and good will have responded not just individually but collectively over the last two and a half decades through three lenses—from Pastor and Ortiz, from Keller, and from our own tri-focal theology—we are able to see some of the ways in which a sustainable movement of city transformation has developed, a movement that, though imperfect and still growing, pictures some of the key principles essential to catalyzing and sustaining transformational city movements in general.

Movement Leadership

I sometimes grow weary of the seemingly endless number of books, articles, podcasts, and blogs describing *leadership* as the key to everything, and for that reason have shied away from pointing to leadership as the easy answer to supporting transformational city movements. But clearly, in Fresno it took no small amount of dedicated and costly leadership in the 1990s to catalyze the transformational city movement here, employing the critical elements we've been discussing. And today, there are still new levels of leadership required to deepen and mature the movement into the ministry ecosystem we've explored. As it turns out, a rubric used by organizational developers has given us perspective about the particular type of leadership required to grow and nurture a transformational city movement. Kouzes and Posner's *Leadership Challenge* (Kouzes & Posner, 2012) is surprisingly descriptive of what has happened in Fresno. And while their framework is primarily concerned with leadership in organizations, we are finding it particularly helpful in its simplicity when cultivating and nurturing leadership capable of growing our movement. For our purposes here it will be helpful to pose a series of questions to that rubric from the perspective of leaders attempting to sustain the movement. Kouzes and Posner identify five disciplines that characterize best practice leadership behavior (Kouzes & Posner, 2003, 73).

Model the Way. Movements must have influencers at the front end who break through the ice of ministry norms and model innovation. The question that leaders who wish to foster city transformation must ask themselves is, "To what extent am I engaged in and centering my work around the goal of creating the beloved community?" It has never been enough in any city to align one's ministry, whether church or nonprofit, incidentally toward "helping people," or "serving people" or offering a program that addresses a particular need – never enough at least to influence lasting change. These piecemeal efforts cannot hope to address the more systemic issues at play in every city. Increasingly, ministries that want to foster a movement toward city transformation must orient their work toward the north star of that goal, and that means leaders have to model it by merging their personal and institutional lives in that direction. In our city, that meant leaders uprooting their families and moving to very poor and very neglected neighborhoods that shocked their friends and colleagues in order to experience them and influence those areas from the inside.

Theologically, this follows an incarnational methodology (John 1:14, Phil 2), the grand relocation of Jesus to become part of the human story, to subject himself to this place of tears, this place of beauty, this fragile, violent, inspiring, heart-ache of a place in order to demonstrate his message of love, embody his commitment to its shalom, and model what the Spirit of God looks like in human form.

Inspire a Shared Vision. As we've noted before a compelling vision is essential, and Kouzes and Posner call us to "envision the future by imagining exciting and ennobling possibilities, and enlist others by appealing to shared hopes, dreams and aspirations" (Kouzes & Posner, 2003, 73). The leader attempting to foster a transformational movement must in this case ask a few questions of him/herself. First, in what arena or sphere have I been given voice to influence the imagination of a city? Second, how broad and deep is my sense of the aspirations of people in my sphere, and how will I augment my understanding of the aspirations of people beyond my sphere? Third, what would I have to re-orient in my responsibilities or re-build in my skillsets to foster a shared vision of the shalom community that God wants to create?

This grows from the biblical vision of community, a view of interrelatedness that is cultivated by a holistic understanding of the human race as God intended it. We call for things to be *as they should be* between people and their God, between people and themselves, between people and each other, and between people and their environment. Transformational Movements call people to that shared vision.

Seek to Contribute. City movements are marked by the spirit of generosity. The authors ask us to consider Fredrick Wilcox's baseball axiom that "you can't steal second with your foot on first" (Kouzes & Posner, 2012, 5). Fostering a movement for city transformation requires risk, innovation, and experimentation with new ministry forms. All of these require at some point a leader who is generous enough to risk what she or he has for the sake of the common good. The two questions leaders must ask themselves in response to this discipline are to what extent have I settled into a pragmatic status quo, with ministry objectives defined more by manageability rather than by the thermometer of how well our most vulnerable populations are faring? And second, what unique resource do I bring to the table of stakeholders that might add value to the transformational process, or the people committed to that process?

Enable others to act. The great tar pit of city transformation—the momentum-stealing, energy-sucking, black hole of institutionalization—is the story of how programs can evolve into sacred cows, becoming synonymous with the identity of an organization. This can leave institutions justifying their existence by preserving and even adding programs. But movements are fed by something more like the energy of an organism rather than by an organization. This is not to say that institutions are not important. Just the opposite. It has been demonstrated just how crucial it is to have a backbone organization that acts as a steward of the institutional relationships and as a vehicle for the common vision in a city in order to build toward a collective impact (Hanleybrown, Kania, and Kramer, 2012, 3). But so many institutions have set their own survival as their primary goal, and therefore their resources go mostly into that effort. Institutions that reorient themselves toward enabling others to act—other organizations, other leaders, other networks—become valued for their ability to hold their own programs lightly in favor of the synergy brought by the coalition. They certainly bring what they have to the table too, but all of the "eggs" of their institutional identity are not in that basket. They become able to link their institutional goals to the collective goals of their collaborative partners in the city. This strengthens the movement, and, perhaps counter-intuitively, strengthens their standing in the community as they allow others to shine.

Encourage the Heart. Finally, I regard Kouzes and Posner's final discipline in the *Leadership Challenge* as being crucial as we examine the movement dynamics of city transformation. Movements have people at their heart. They are not merely the result of cold calculation or strategic planning. When emerging leaders take an onramp to civic engagement they do so because of others on that pathway, because they link their personal aspirations and longings to the well-being of the city, and because they internally believe that they "will find their peace in the peace of the city" (Jer 29:7).This requires recognition, celebration, and a sense of the onramp community that has been formed.

Transformational movements are born out of a commitment to take stock of our assets, to build on our strengths, and to mobilize people of faith and people of good will in building the kind of future that honors the dignity of every human being, whom we know to be created in the image of God. Movements are born when people of good faith working with people of good will get exposed to creative, viable models and are given the freedom to tailor and experiment inside their sphere of influence. Long-term transformational influence is the result of "disciplined practices that are consistent with movement" (Woodward & White, 2016, 12).

Christ-Centered Civic Transformation

Leaders in our city exhibit a rare understanding that our individual efforts – no matter how noble or well-intended – cannot produce the kind of systemic transformation necessary in a a region. But we have also learned that this level of *unified identity leading to a purpose* flies in the face of American individualistic strategies, and the cult of leadership and personality that is so often the default. Cities will always revert to that mode if a culture of collective impact is not nurtured. And as long as city transformation efforts are the mere initiative of a few leaders, rather than the product of a self-nurturing, self-sustaining, broad-based movement, they will make little progress toward the beloved community for which we all long.

What Fresno has in common with the Abolitionists of the 1800s, the Women's Suffrage Movement of the early 1900s, the Civil Rights Movement of the 1960s, and South Africa's Anti-Apartheid Movement of the 1990s is not the history-making impact, but the same values, frameworks, components, and strategies that make for sustainable, transformational outcomes over time. Igniting social change in the name of Jesus Christ in ways that catalyze ongoing, sustainable spiritual and social transformation in cities is possible. I am happy to say, Fresno is becoming a quiet, unpretentious example of just such a movement.

Works Cited

DeYmaz and Li, (2010). *Ethnic Blends: Mixing Diversity into Your Local Church (Leadership Network Innovation Series)*. Grand Rapids, MI: Zondervan.

Gladwell, Malcomb, (2002). *The Tipping Point: How Little Things Can Make a Big Difference*, Boston, MA: Back Bay Books.

Hanleybrown, Fay, and Kania, John, and Kramer, Mark, (January 2012). Channeling Change: Making Collective Impact Work. *Stanford Innovation Review.*

James M. Kouzes & Barry Z. Posner, (2003). *"The Five Practices of Exemplary Leadership."* San Francisco, CA: Pfeiffer, A Wiley Imprint.

James M. Kouzes & Barry Z. Posner, (2012). *The Leadership Challenge*, San Francisco, CA: Jossey-Bass.

Keller, Timothy, (2012). *Center Church: Doing Balanced, Gospel Centered Ministry in Your City*, Grand Rapids MI: Zondervan.

Keller, Timothy, (2011). *To Transform a City*, Leadership Journal, http://www.christianitytoday.com/le/2011/winter/transformcity.html

New Bible Dictionary, (1962). Leicester, England: Tyndale House Publishers, InterVarsity Press,

Pastoral, Manuel, Ortiz, Rhonda, (2009, March). *Making Change: How Social Movements Work and How to Support Them,* https://dornsife.usc.edu/pere/ making-change/ (accessed 9-26-16)

White, Randy, Ed., (2012). *The Work of Our Hands: Faith Rooted Approaches to Job Creation, Job Training, or Job Placement in a Context of Concentrated Poverty,* Condeopress.com

Woodward, JR., & White, Dan, Jr., (2016). *The Church as Movement: Starting and Sustaining Missional-Incarnational Communities*, Downers Grover, IL: InterVarsity Press.

Yoder, Perry, (1987). *Shalom: The Bible's Word for Salvation, Justice and Peace*, Nappanee, IN: Evangel Press,

Chapter Three

A Christ-Centered Approach to Community Organizing Across Ethnic, Cultural and Faith Sectors

Bryson White

Faith in Fresno/PICO

Many and varied are the interpretations dealing with the teachings and the life of Jesus of Nazareth. But few of these interpretations deal with what the teachings and the life of Jesus have to say to those who stand, at a moment in human history, with their back against the wall.

Howard Thurman

The masses of men live with their backs constantly against the wall. They are poor, the disinherited, the dispossessed. What does our religion say to them? The issue is not what it counsels them to do for others whose need may be greater, but what religion offers to meet their own needs. The search for an answer to this question is perhaps the most important religious quest of modern life."

Howard Thurman

In Fresno, California, a group of pastors, lay leaders, and community organizers set out to listen to their community to understand what was driving the gun violence in the area. A team of people would walk through neighborhoods that were affected by gun violence and simply have conversations with neighbors, then document what residents saw as issues in their neighborhood that they wanted to see addressed by the city. I was part of this group that became known as "Fresno Nightwalks," led by Reverend B.T. Lewis, the Pastor of Rising Star Missionary Baptist Church. We would walk neighborhoods each Friday evening and ask people we encountered, "What do you like about your neighborhood?" and "What would you like to see changed?" Although we started our walks as a way of addressing gun violence in the area, we were transformed by hearing residents talk to us about things that were right in front of us but that our eyes could not see—the massive amount of abandoned properties in the city.

One Friday evening while walking through the neighborhood I approached a few children who were playing in front of their home. I asked one of the young girls the two questions and she responded she did not like the three abandoned and boarded-up homes across the street from her house. She said they made her feel bad and made her not want to play outside. This young girl knew these abandoned properties changed the way her neighborhood looked and felt. After the young lady opened our eyes to what was right in front of us, we ended up counting 30 abandoned properties throughout her entire neighborhood—a neighborhood which is only a half-mile across.

After our conversation with the young girl, we began to hear more and more from residents about the problem of abandoned and blighted properties, not only in this particular neighborhood where we were walking, but across the several neighborhoods where "Fresno Nightwalks" had spread. Our organization, Faith In Community, in partnership with the Sociology Department at Fresno State University identified nearly 10,000 vacant and boarded-up properties within the city.

Through the actions of a few clergy connecting with the pain surrounding their congregations, we were able to identify a key problem in our city and begin to create solutions for alleviating this issue. Through the process of community organizing we were able to get the city to pass an ordinance that required property owners to register vacant homes with the city after sixty days and maintain yards and exteriors in good conditions, forbid them from covering windows and entries with plywood, leveraged hefty fines on owners who violated these rules. This did not alleviate the issue of slum property owners; Faith In Community, in a coalition with community partners, continues to work on housing equity to create a Fresno where all residents can live in housing worthy of their inherent human dignity. However, this process does highlight that congregations, through connecting with the residents in their parish neighborhood, can not only hear the grievances of the community, but can in fact work in a way that brings resolution to community grievances.

Methodology

This chapter will focus on the role that community organizing plays in creating a pathway for people of the Christian faith to become involved in the *missio Dei* by connecting their faith to civic engagement. I will proffer that community organizing is a vital tool for the Church to use in order for us to deepen our understanding of how our faith can be active in the world, for renewing the faith of parishioners, and for standing with those with their backs against the wall. Community organizing will be situated within the broader missionary activity of the Church within the *missio dei*, and will be rooted in an analysis of the life of Jesus and the missionary activity of the early church. Furthermore, I will sketch some of the key components to faith-based community organizing such as the cycle of community organizing, clergy formation and decision making, and cross-cultural components to organizing.

God's Encounter with the World

When we read the Bible we encounter a God who is engaging the world in history by both mighty supernatural deeds as well as by empowering God's people to engage the world in new and fresh ways. As Christians reflect on the person, nature, and activity of God we develop particular worldviews to understand God's activity in the world based upon our social, cultural, and historical contexts. Thus, Christian theology is varied, layered, and textured and it is not a neutral enterprise—meaning it looks at the world through the lens of Christian faith and also cannot be narrowly defined. Missiology, a branch of Christian theology, must also not be narrowly defined and reduced to one particular understanding or expression. According to Missiologist David J. Bosch, "The most we can hope for is to formulate some approximations of what mission is all about" (Bosch, 1996, 9). Furthermore, Bosch states that "Christian mission gives expression to the dynamic relationship between God and the world, particularly as this was portrayed, first, in the story of the covenant people of Israel and then, supremely, in the birth, life, death, resurrection, and exaltation of Jesus of Nazareth" (Bosch, 1996, 9).

It is important to distinguish between two key terms in the world of missiology: *mission* (singular) and *missions* (plural). I find it useful to continue to use the work of missiologist David. J. Bosch to interpret these terms for us. The term *missio Dei* (God's mission) refers to God's self-revelation as the One who loves the world, God's involvement in and with the world, and the nature and activity of God which embraces both the church and the world and in which the Church is privileged to participate (Bosch, 1996, 10). The term *missions* (the missionary ventures of the Church or *missio ecclesia*) refer to particular forms, related to specific times, places, or needs, of participation in the *missio Dei*. Christian theologies are a byproduct of the missionary ventures of the Church, contrary to popular thought. Christian theology in its origins was not born in a vacuum, detached from the struggle to interpret the meaning of the birth, life, death, and resurrection of Jesus. The New Testament writers were writing in the heat of the Church's encounter with the world as well as encountering one another, and in this context they were forced to engage the discipline of theology. David Bosch rightly puts it that the New Testament writers were not scholars who had the leisure to research before they put paper to pen, but rather, they were writing in the context of an "emergency situation" and were forced to theologize (Bosch, 1996, 16). This concept of an "emergency situation" I will revisit later in this chapter, as a window through which we can peer into the necessity of community organizing as a vital component of God's mission in contemporary America.

Jesus and Mission

The life of the church is supposed to be shaped and informed by the life of Jesus, both through his physical life and teachings that we encounter in the Gospels, as well as his life as he moves in and amongst the Church contemporarily. As we engage in this chapter, concepts of the *missio Dei* and how community organizing can serve as a tool for the *missio ecclesia,* it would behoove us to talk briefly about how Jesus understood his mission in his historical context. For the vast majority of Christians in the United States the person of Jesus is understood to be a benign and non-confrontational historical figure whose chief concern is getting people into heaven and is not engaged in improving the material conditions of the lives of people. This interpretation of the life and teachings of Jesus has had obvious effects on the way the church has understood its mission to proclaim the one who came to save the world. However, this is not how Jesus understood his own earthly mission. Here I want to introduce the work of biblical scholar Obery Hendricks and his classic text *The Politics of Jesus* as a guide for us to learn from the inaugural sermon of Jesus. By "politics" Hendricks does not mean that Jesus sought to bring about another "protest party" in Galilee, nor that he was "involved in politics" in the sense in which we understand contemporary American politics and its accompanying discourse. Nor does he mean that Jesus wanted to overthrow the Roman Empire by force. Rather, Jesus being political means that not only did he call for changed individual hearts but for also sweeping and comprehensive change in the political, social, and economic structures in his setting in life—that is, colonized Israel (Hendricks, 2006, 4). According to Hendricks, Jesus being political means that if he had it his way the ruling powers would either have to vacate their positions of power, or rule in a completely different fashion (Hendricks, 2006, 4).

Let's turn to Jesus's inaugural sermon as a window into how Jesus understood his mission:

> The Spirit of the Lord is upon me, because he has anointed me to bring good news to the poor. He has sent me to proclaim release to the captives, and recovery of sight to the blind, to let the oppressed go free, to proclaim the year of the Lord's favor" (Luke 4:18–19).

In the Gospel of Luke we find Jesus's inaugural sermon highlighting that the reason for his anointing by God and the purpose of his mission in the world are one and the same. According to Obery Hendricks, Jesus leaves no doubt to his radical calling in his inaugural sermon because he does three things. First, he heralded good news to the poor, or *ptochois*—the Greek word for poor indicating a collective or class identity (Hendricks, 2006, 7). Jesus grounded his mission as one that struggles for change of the circumstances and institutions that kept people downtrodden and impoverished, because it is only through a radical change, or more aptly put, a radical re-ordering of society, that the material conditions for the poor can change. Second, Jesus announces release to the captives—that is, to those *unjustly imprisoned*—which was aimed directly at the Roman jails that were full of political prisoners and those reduced to penury by economic exploitation (Hendricks, 2006, 7). Hendricks declares that Jesus then takes his pronouncement a step further by announcing *"liberation to those who were oppressed"* by the crushing weight of the Roman Empire. The Greek word for "oppressed" is *thrawo* meaning to "oppress, crush." The capstone to Jesus's inaugural sermon is his proclaiming of the "acceptable year of the Lord," an illusion to the year of Jubilee when all land that had been confiscated or unjustly acquired was to be returned to its original owners (Lev 25:8–10). For Obery Hendricks, the inaugural sermon of Jesus illustrates that he understood his anointing by God and his mission to Israel as one of a divine appointment to struggle for—to *"bring"*—economic, political, and social justice to his people (Hendricks, 2004, 7).

Another illustration of Jesus's mission being inclusive of the material reality which people inhabit daily is in the "Lord's Prayer." Here we find Jesus instructing his disciples that whenever they pray, their first concern should be that Caesar's unjust governance (as manifested in imperial policies and laws) and unjust will be replaced by the just governance and the just will of God (*thy kingdom come, thy will be done*) (Hendricks, 2006, 7). The consummate teacher, Jesus makes sure his disciples understand that these instructions were not meant to be understood merely as abstract theories—so he carefully added *"on earth as in heaven."* It was radical statements like these that were considered high treason against the Roman state and ultimately led to Jesus's execution. Returning to the work of Bosch we find that many of the early Christian sayings and attitudes, building off of the mission of Jesus, were outright seditious during the period of the early church, yet we no longer experience them as such—this applies not only to the Jesus movement but also to Paul, Luke, and other New Testament writers (Bosch, 1996, 47). The primary difference, however, between the "political seditiousness" and the "revolutionary" language of the early church and that of the world is that the measurements were not and should not be the same. "Worldly" revolution is measured by how much terror one can inflict, while the Jesus movement is measured by the alternatives it has to offer (Bosch, 1996, 47). The early church was deeply political in the sense that it rejected all gods and in doing so demolished the metaphysical foundations of prevailing political theories—this is primarily expressed in announcing Jesus as Lord of lords which is the most revolutionary political demonstration imaginable in the Roman Empire of the first centuries of the Christian era (Bosch, 1996, 47). Both Hendricks and Bosch help us understand that the idea of religion as a private affair and divorcing the spiritual from the physical is antithetical to the reign of God that Jesus proclaimed in his inaugural sermon in Luke, through many other acts and deeds recorded in the Gospel narratives, and in the life of the early church.

Having established that the life of Jesus ushered in an understanding of salvation that is both personal and social, and that the early church was also a spiritual/political reality, we now turn to how community organizing can serve as a tool to aid the church in reconnecting with a more comprehensive and accurate understanding of its mission and be used as a tool to improve the material conditions of those who, like Jesus, are deeply marginalized by ungodly power structures.

Essential Elements to Community Organizing: The Cycle

At the heart of faith-based community organizing are personal relationships with those who have their backs against the wall. Entering into or deepening pre-existing relationships allows for two people to share their griefs, struggles, and hopes with one another—and to activate one another into a mode of action to contribute gifts and talents to the transformation of a person's community. This relational space is called a "one-to-one." In a one-to-one an organizer or a community leader within an organization meets with someone in the community who has been recommended by a clergy person, another leader within the organization, or a community partner, to think deeply about what the person cares most about. A critical question that a community organizer or faith leader might ask in this context is, "Who do you love?" This question is critical as it takes the conversation to a place of depth and allows for the organizer/faith leader to hear the heart of the leader they are meeting with, while also allowing for the organizer/faith leader to share who they are as a person. When we think about who we love, we also think about what brings them joy and what brings them pain and grief. It is in hearing the pain and grief of a person that we enter into their world, and person by person begin to reweave the social fabric of a city.

Furthermore, as the leader begins to open up about the pain his or her loved ones are experiencing, we are able to begin to think together about theology—how they understand God's engagement with the world, or what they believe God wants for the world. In this process we are able to hear how faith plays an active role in the life of the leader and begin to think critically about how that faith is a tool for moving from a privatized expression to one where it becomes active in the lives of others. In this setting we can begin to think about other people we should reach out to together, both new people as well as pre-existing social networks, in order to begin building a structure that can channel the people power we are amassing. Social scientists call this "building social capital." However, the social capital being amassed is laden with moral-ethical and political meaning. It is social capital to be spent on behalf of love and justice versus what it is normally used to accumulate—wealth.

A good one-to-one will lead to connecting with other people within the person's pre-existing social network in a congregation. If an organizer has a series of successful one-to-ones, and participants want to continue thinking critically about how they can resolve an issue, then a team is formed. Forming a team is critical in community organizing. It is here where people together share concerns about issues and pressures they are facing, things the organizer may have heard about in the one-to-one. After sharing concerns it is the team that together picks an issue they feel is critical to alleviating a particular pressure affecting their family. These issues can range from smaller, more manageable issues such as the need for more stop signs in their neighborhood, to more complex issues such as payday lending or police accountability. It is within this space that the organizer is tasked with training the team on how to use their gifts in particular ways to bring about a change within a particular system that will alleviate the issue. A team meeting usually consists of a faith reflection from a sacred text, a credential (a shared statement of what the organization or this particular group stands for), a testimony by a leader to share how the process of organizing is impacting his or her personal life, and a training by the organizer or leader regarding a key component of community organizing. It is in the team setting that we move from a problem to an issue, as a problem is something that is named, but an issue is something that can be worked on to be alleviated.

In order for the team to tackle an issue in a way that achieves results, team members need to understand the issue they want to address. This requires detailed research. This research phase comprises of but is not limited to finding out what other cities have done to address the issue and having both public and private research meetings with experts (public officials, nonprofits, professors, etc.) regarding the issue of concern. In these spaces it allows for leaders to ask key questions, present counter information, flesh out the depth of the issue, and most importantly step into a deeper level of their leadership by becoming more comfortable being in front of "powerful" people.

Following the research phase and after gaining a clear understanding of the issue and solutions that can be proffered to alleviate it, leaders may choose to hold a public "action" to secure a public agreement with a public official to begin to change the issue. These actions are really key to leadership development as they enable community leaders to put forth a public narrative that is often contrary to the narrative of the powerful that shapes public policy decisions. It also allows leaders from the community to step into their power by reversing the roles of power in a public space. A public official, typically seen as the most important person in the room, is instead seen as secondary to the leaders from the community and the concerns they are lifting up. In terms of Christian theological language this is a small example of the first being last and the last being first—as it seeks to show that those without power in fact do have power and are equal to those with established power. Richard Wood (Wood, 2002, 42) aptly describes "public actions" as "public dramas," because they are designed with a *dramaturgical* emphasis on drawing participants into the political tension of public life and using the energy of the crowd to push the drama of public decision making into democratic directions. A public action can be space where an elected official is held accountable, or a space where they report the good work they have done in partnership with the community organization.

An Example of Public Action: California Assembly Bill AB953

On September 12th, 2015 a coalition of diverse religious and community leaders comprised of First Nations, African-American, Latino, Caucasian, and Asian peoples descended on the state capitol of California to declare a new reality—one where the dignity of all people will be respected by law enforcement. The context for this gathering was the pain people of color in California have been experiencing at the hands of law enforcement due to racial profiling. This multi-racial and multi-faith coalition of people went to Sacramento to encourage and demand Governor Brown to sign AB953 into law, a bill that would both require the State of California to expand its definition of identity profiling as well as require law enforcement agencies across California to document the identity of the person they have pulled over. This day of "action" was organized by a coalition of faith and identity-based community organizing organizations from across California, with representation from both the metropolitan and rural areas of the state.

The day was broken into three parts: testimony, visits to officials holding state office, and protest. The testimony portion of the day consisted of Christian pastors connecting the Gospel of Jesus to the creation of public policy that values the life of the vulnerable; in this instance, that values the lives of people of color disproportionately affected by racial profiling. Testimonies from First Nations peoples consisted of detailing the untimely death of unarmed loved ones at the hands of law enforcement. A spokesperson from Asian-Americans Advancing Justice lifted up the need for Asian sisters and brothers to not allow for the model minority stereotype to continue contributing to division amongst people of color. Latino and African-American leaders shared stories that detailed their experiences with racial profiling and the distrust towards law enforcement it has created in their communities. This was a sacred space, crafted to ground the day in two key elements: the faith of the people, and the pain of the people. It was designed to show that the Gospel of Jesus has something to say to those with their backs up against the wall.

The second portion of the day consisted of joining local teams to visit our elected representatives and encourage them to pass the legislation through the State Senate. However, the most important part of the "action" is when hundreds of people gathered in the hallway in front of the Governor's office encouraging him to do the moral thing and sign the bill into law. It was in this space that the multi-racial and multi-faith component of community organizing came to bear. White pastors locked arms with black and Latino Pastors, Latino and black lay leaders locked arms with white and Asia Pacific Island lay leaders in an act of civil disobedience. A sacred space was intentionally created that allowed for people to enter into the pain of their neighbor, not in an abstract or theoretical sense, but in concrete terms where people put their bodies on the line in an act of prophetic disobedience—prepared to go to jail on behalf of the life of their neighbor.

This was a sacred space. Testimonies of pain created at the hands of law enforcement were lifted, freedom songs were sung, and biblical Scriptures were recited in unison by hundreds of people in a crammed hallway at the state capitol directly in front of the Governor's office. This was a direct action to tell the Governor of the State of California to sign AB953 into law and begin to curb racial and identity profiling in California. There were two powerful currents that merged in that hallway. The first was that marginalized people, primarily people of color from across the state, came to the center of power to declare their humanity and to influence the democratic process. The second was that Caucasian pastors were able to enter into the pain of people of color and not only stand in solidarity with but also risk their bodies in this solidarity. In the hallway of the powerful in Sacramento a sacred space was created, where the vulnerable were highlighted and not moved to the side, where the powerful were following the lead of the vulnerable, where human beings typically divided by race, gender, faith, and culture were able to enter into the pain of each other and declare a new reality. Governor Brown had declared that it would take an "act of God" to sign this bill into law—he signed the bill into law on Saturday October 3rd, 2015. The act of God he was looking for came to the Capitol in the form of a multi-racial group of people who understood Howard Thurman's interpretation of the message of Jesus—that our faith has to say something to those with their back against wall.

The end result of the process of community organizing is based on a few transformational components. The first is how have the leaders in the organization been transformed by the process of sharing their pain, doing detailed research, and being in front of and holding elected officials responsible? How do they understand the role of their faith in this process? How has their faith deepened or become more practical? Secondly, what tangible change has occurred from the work the leaders have done from a policy standpoint? Has there been a policy or operational change within the target institution that will lead to the improved lives of marginalized peoples? If the answer to the second component is no, then the campaign is incomplete—it is not a failure, but the particular goal has not been met, which requires reconvening and thinking about new directions to bring about the change that is sought.

One of the ways an organization can think about new directions to bring about change is the tactic of escalation through direct action. The direct action taken at the state capitol in Sacramento was not the first step in engaging the issue; it came after research meetings with the Governor's staff did not produce the results we needed to see. Direct action emerges as a way of disrupting the process of day-to-day business at a particular target location or geographic area. Regarding AB 953 it was at the state capitol; for Black Lives Matter protestors across the country that disruption has included freeways or commercial districts. Direct action creates a larger narrative around the issue and forces government entities, private business, or residents to confront the reality of the pain that marginalized people feel.

Direct action is central to the story of our nation's history, from the Boston Tea Party throwing boxes of imported British tea into the Atlantic, or Martin Luther King Jr. leading the Montgomery Bus Boycott to usher in the Civil Rights Movement, to the current Black Lives Matter protestors who target government spaces as well as freeways and shopping malls to bring the business of the city to a halt and lift up grievances.

Key Components to Multi-Faith Community Organizing

In the previous paragraphs I have sought to illustrate how the church is called to be a part of God's mission, which includes understanding how Jesus understood his own mission. Furthermore, I briefly detailed the cycle of community organizing as a way to participate in God's mission, reconnect people to their faith, activate lay leadership, bring people into the democratic process, and forge new ways for social policies that enhance the lives of marginalized people. I also shared a story about how public action creates a space to hold public officials accountable to the people they were elected to govern. Now I would like to engage the role of clergy in community organizing, but particularly the way in which clergy across various faith contexts make shared decisions regarding the movement of the organization they are involved in.

The role of the pastor or clergy leader in faith-based organizing is critical. While pastors, deacons, organizers, and lay leaders all bring particular authority into organizing, clergy carry the most power. Clergy can bring legitimacy to your organizing efforts by giving you access to their congregation, identifying leaders, allowing you to make announcements, addressing an issue through the lens of sacred text, forming congregational teams to further the work, and recruiting other clergy. Clergy can also delegitimize an organization by choosing to not do any of these things. One of the greatest obstacles for clergy involvement, particularly for male evangelical clergy, is the suspicion of being in spaces that are not completely Christian, or in spaces with other Christian clergy who do not share evangelical interpretations of Scripture. One of the key issues that can drive a wedge within a multi-denominational or multi-faith clergy caucus is the tenseness regarding gender issues.

I have had several conversations with evangelical clergy who were weary of working with mainline Protestant clergy who performed same-sex marriage ceremonies. One clergy person in particular told me outright that he would not join our clergy caucus because two of our prominent clergy performed same-gender wedding ceremonies. I explained to this clergy person that the reality is that our organization does not work on wedge issues such as same-sex marriage or abortion/women's reproductive rights because we understand that if we took a stance one way or another regarding these issues that our coalition would be in danger of falling apart. Furthermore, we can't do anything regarding those issues locally anyway. This conversation did not end well, as the person did not believe that he should be in fellowship with clergy who held a theological position opposed to his, so he decided to not join our fellowship.

Conversations like these are critical, because in order to do effective faith-based organizing, you need to know what you want to accomplish. Not everyone will be on board with that vision, and that's okay. It's not about selling a product to a clergy person, but instead it's about seeing whether or not our visions align with one another in terms of how our faith traditions are calling us to be active in the world.

One of the places the creation of shared vision exists is a local clergy caucus comprised of clergy within your organization. The clergy caucus is a gathering of clergy from different faith contexts with an aim of creating a space of relationship building, training, and decision-making. The culture of a caucus is predicated upon clergy being able to engage other clergy through their own faith and theological lenses, without feeling they need to "convert" to another faith tradition, nor be in a defensive posture about their religious beliefs. The basic structure of a caucus is leading with a faith reflection, a discussion regarding a particular issue campaign, and training by an organizer on community organizing and team formation. Once clergy who are committed to the work of justice feel comfortable that they are not required to check their faith tradition at the door, entering into relationships with other clergy from different doctrinal commitments and faith contexts becomes much easier. In order for this to be accomplished, however, there are particular issues and stances that the caucus will not collectively take a stance on. Issues such as same-gender marriage, abortion, and Israeli-Palestine conflicts are left fully outside of the space of the caucus due to their divisive nature. In their own space, clergy may affirm or oppose same-gender marriage or abortion, but in the shared space of the caucus there is never a public stance in favor of or against these issues. Instead, energies are directed at issues that can be resolved primarily at the local level and at times the state level.

The diversity of faith and ethnicity within the clergy of a faith-based organization can and does lead to different understandings regarding the way the organization interacts with public officials. For instance, due to the climate of xenophobia and religious bigotry in our country, a rabbi may have a different relationship with the police department than an Anglo liberal mainline protestant pastor does. This is because synagogues are faced with constant threats of violence and rely on the police department more heavily for protection. In contrast, an Anglo liberal mainline Protestant pastor is typically not under any threats of violence (though this is not always the case) and may be able to take a more critical stance towards law enforcement. Furthermore, the terrain that a Muslim cleric navigates is complicated due to the xenophobia and the subsequent threats from the public that follow which create a situation where they, too, need the protection from law enforcement and may be less apt to publically criticize the activity of law enforcement officials. In addition to the world that non-Christians navigate, the racial atmosphere of our country creates another potential point of tension in a multi-faith and multi-racial context. For instance, what happens when a sheriff or a police chief are promoting policies that disproportionately affect minority communities and when African-American clergy speak with a more critical voice towards these institutions? These situations become tough to navigate, as people from different communities have varying relationships with law enforcement, thus holding to differing understandings of engagement with them from a critical standpoint. Through this, relationships have to be strong enough to navigate the decision making process in a pluralistic context.

Navigating Clergy Relationships

During a public action in the Summer of 2015, our organization brought the Regional U.S. Attorney of the Department of Justice to be part of a Town Hall meeting with our chief of police and district attorney. The point of this Town Hall was twofold; to lift up concerns regarding the activities of local law enforcement, and to create a community policing structure in the Fresno Police Department as outlined by President Obama's 21st Century Policing Taskforce. During the event, one of our key white mainline Protestant clergy critiqued the district attorney on some of the comments she made. While the critique was accurate, a few key African-American clergy within our organization interpreted it as harsh and unnecessary. What this event revealed is there were different understandings of what holding elected officials accountable means for the organization and factors such as race, city-cultural context, and geographic location had much to do with shaping the varied perspectives.

One of the key principles of community organizing is, "When in doubt have a one-on-one", so I had a series of one-on-ones with parties involved in response to the internal crisis. I discovered that for the white mainline Protestant clergy person, what he said in the moment was accurate and thus should have been said regardless of whether or not it was "on script" or not. Furthermore, the conversation with this clergy person revealed that he thought the organization was "uncritically" engaging with the chief of police, particularly because at the time we were not calling for his resignation. He understood this stance as our organization not acting within the prophetic tradition of which we claimed to be a part. This person's intentions were honest in his understandings of what it means to both hold public officials accountable and declare a new vision for our city.

However, two of the African-American clergy persons leading this particular action felt his actions were reckless and unneeded. From their vantage points, by the time of this clergy person's actions we had already received the commitments we wanted, namely, a commitment by the police department to implement 21st Century Community Policing tactics as outlined by President Obama's Task Force on Policing. Furthermore, one-on-ones with both African-American clergy persons revealed that although they held criticisms of the chief of police they did not think asking for his resignation was the best course of action if he was in agreement to implement our policy recommendations. In addition to this, they were upset about the situation because they believed that if they were to take a public stance of this sort it would create a situation where they were "speaking for the entire community," and they felt this would be an unfair stance to take. Meanwhile, the comments or actions taken by the mainline Protestant clergy would be attributed to him solely and not to his community at large. Both of their intentions were also honest in their understandings of what it means to both hold public officials accountable and declare a new vision for our city.

As the organizer in the situation, I understood both sides of the argument. On the one hand, a part of being bold and prophetic is asking for the resignation of public officials if the community in fact believes they have violated public trust. One the other hand, for some, when you are pastoring an underserved community it may lead you to believe that you need access to the power structure of the city to get change implemented. What I stressed in the situation was the restoring of trust towards one another, for both sides to believe that their stance was rooted in the concern for the community and city. However, trust has not been fully restored between the offended parties. What the situation created, however, was an opportunity for the organization to begin to think deeply about who we are and how we are going to function together in the public space. We began to answer questions such as, "What does being bold mean? What is our relationship to the power structure of the city going to be?" It also made us think about how we are becoming "gatekeepers" in the city sitting at an already prepared table, instead of calling for the creation of a new table entirely. It created an internal conversation amongst clergy and staff to answer the question, " In what ways are we acting as the "chaplain to empire" and in what ways do we need to act as "prophets of resistance"?

Forming relationships with one another is the only way clergy can build a consensus in a religiously pluralistic organization. By entering into the relationship with one another, others can begin to see the pain communities may be in. Through this realization, clergy begin to stand with one another based upon a pain that neither they nor any other person in their congregation may have experienced. The path forward in public engagement where people have different viewpoints becomes based upon those closest to the pain of the problem. According to Moral Theologian Meghan Clark, this organizing principle is called *Subsidiarity*, which is an "effort at balancing the many levels of society— and at its best, the principle of *subsidiarity* navigates the allocation of resources by higher levels of society to support the engagement and decision making by the lower levels (of society)" (Clark, Meghan, 2012). In essence, those closet to the pain need to dictate both the process and outcomes of the work of justice.

Faith-based organizing is key to creating healthy neighborhoods and cities. It is a work that is rooted first in the *Missio Dei*, as well as in relationship building through encountering one another in new and transformative ways. It is a process that includes one-on-ones with congregants, pastors, and residents, participating in deep research with public officials and policy experts, and planning and executing public accountability sessions with public officials. Crucial to the work of organizing is re-imagining who matters in the public square, decentering those with power and privilege, and putting those at the margins at the center of our concerns. It is difficult work, which I hope that I have communicated in this chapter, as it entails navigating different theological visions, social location, personalities, and deeply rooted structures of power that benefit the strong and limit the vulnerable. However, this work is much needed if the Church is going to live at the intersection of faith and justice in this current generation and generations to come.

Works Cited

Bosch, David, (1996). *Transforming Mission: Paradigm Shifts in Theology of Mission*, Maryknoll, NY: Orbis Books

Clark, Meghan. (2012). March 8. *Subsidiarity Is A Two-Sided Coin* [Web log post] *Retrieved from* http://catholicmoraltheology.com/subsidiarity-is-a-two-sided-coin/)

Hendricks, Obery, (2004). *The Politics of Jesus: Rediscovering the True Revolutionary Nature of Jesus' Teachings and How They Have Been Corrupted*, New York, NY: Doubleday Publishing.

Thurman, Howard, (1976). *Jesus and the Disinherited*, Boston, MA: Beacon Press.

Wood, Richard, (2002). *Faith in Action: Religion, Race, and Demographic Organizing in America*, Chicago, IL: University of Chicago Press.

Chapter Four

Fostering a Culture of Multi-Sector Alliance in Your City

Cathleen Lawler

Clovis Christian Church

> *"To bear fruit, compassion must give birth to strategy."*
>
> Rusau & Swanson

As a community-oriented practitioner, my curiosity was ignited several years ago as I read an article in our local paper about the birth of a food pantry coalition. It began when leaders from The City of Clovis, an affluent community adjacent to the more urban Fresno, and the Business Organization of Old Town Clovis (BOOT) teamed up to combat the city's growing hunger problem with a goal of pooling resources to provide food for those who needed it most. At the City's initiative, BOOT helped develop this NOSH program, a word meaning a snack or light meal, "to provide, to nourish, and to give" fruits and vegetables to families in need (Lawson-Swezey, 2014, 1). A representative of the city called churches in the community who were known to have food pantries and listed a phone number to call for further information. So we got our church added to the Friday night rotation of food pantry recipients of donated produce. The city led, the church responded, and a cross-sector partnership was born.

We are not just given the produce, but each Friday night the food pantry representatives sit at a table in the middle of the farmers market produce block and share with customers walking by about the NOSH program which encourages shoppers to purchase extra produce from vendors and donate it to the food pantry. At the end of the evening, many of the vendors also donate some of the leftover produce. The food pantries express their gratitude to the farmers and vendors but many of the vendors express their gratitude for what the food pantries do for the community. When I thanked one of the Asian vendors for her generous donation, she responded with, "No, thank *you*. We are so grateful that this food goes to people who are in need. We have no way of doing this. If it wasn't for you, we would have to throw a lot of this away. So we are happy to make this available so you can give it to people who need help."

Cross-sector collaboration and diverse coalitions that are flexible and sustainable can respond to changing community needs and political landscapes. "Working together provides opportunities to achieve results we are more likely to achieve together than alone" (Winer & Ray, 1996, x).

What is different about our church's food distribution from the other food pantries is that we don't take it in-house to add to our staple items. Rather, on Saturday mornings we deliver it to low-income mobile home parks and apartments. These are pocket areas the City had identified as the most in need. These populations rarely spend their limited dollars on fresh produce. When we started taking food to these locations, we had no clue this was the start of a great collaboration; collaboration between our church, farmers market vendors, businesses, city leaders, other churches, and mobile home park and apartment building dwellers. And the list of those involved continues to grow. Working together provides opportunities to achieve greater results than we can achieve by working alone.

More work and resources are needed to transform a city than can possibly be imagined by one entity. Partnering with others in the city who share concerns is essential. In their book, *Forces for Good*, authors Leslie

Crutchfield and Heather Grant claim that collaboration with others is not one of the characteristics of high-impact nonprofit organizations, but rather it is essential to all practices. They write, "The secret to success lies in how great organizations mobilize every sector of society—government, business, nonprofits, and the public—to be a force for good.... Great organizations work with and through others to create more impact than they could ever achieve alone" (Crutchfield and Grant, 2008, 19).

Cooperation and collaboration are not the same. In their research on the topic, Roschelle and Teasley (1995, 70) describe cooperative work as a task that is accomplished by dividing it among participants, where "each person is responsible for a portion of the problem solving," and they see collaborative work as "the mutual engagement of participants in a coordinated effort to solve the problem together." The key difference between these approaches to working together is that cooperation is more focused on working together to create an end product, while successful collaboration requires participants to share in the process of data collection and the creation of the process and results. In other words, cooperation can be achieved if all participants do their assigned parts separately and bring their results to the table; collaboration, in contrast, implies direct interaction among individuals to produce results and involves negotiations, discussions, and accommodation of others' perspectives.

Collaboration provides an opportunity and invokes a challenge to bring people together in ways that result in more than the sum of individuals. Bringing together diverse stakeholders, melding their resources, and stretching their minds to embrace new ideas and a new vision is essential to civic transformation. "Collaboration is the most intense way of working together while still retaining the separate identities of the organizations involved. The beauty of collaboration is the acknowledgement that each organization has a separate and special function, a power that it brings to the joint effort" (Winer & Ray, 1996, 23). The mutual goal is the achievement of community benefits.

The Church as a Stakeholder

God cares about every person, and he values each and every city. He has commissioned the church, his body, to communicate that truth to each person in every city. To do so effectively, the church in any locality needs to be united as Jesus prayed it would be. "The body of Christ is more than a single local congregation in a community" (Barth, 2010, 166). As we, the church, increase our impact in serving the community through collaboration, we increase our witness, and those who are served take notice. Collaboration produces a city movement, and Barth further explains "a city movement gives us the opportunity to break out of the homogeneous unit principle and demonstrate oneness that crosses the barriers of race, gender, generation, and socioeconomic class."

God can transform a city from a state of near death and decay to a place of physical, economic, emotional, and spiritual health through his people united with a corporate vision. "God's balanced church, working together in mission, is the last thing Satan and his underworld want to see," proclaims Halter & Smay (2010, 156). Unity is vital as Christians work to inhabit the promised lands of their cities.

No single ministry, organization, or church can ever hope to transform its city; the forces at work are far too complex and the scale too large. "Only the Church as a whole can reach an entire city" (Dennison, 1999, 97). Every segment of the faith community is needed to contribute to transforming a community. Collaboration with other sectors of the community is vital as well.

There are theological reasons for embarking on a collaborative mission to reach the community and minister to the many needs of those living there. Rusaw and Swanson name one in *The Externally Focused Church*: "Service is the only location that encompasses the needs and dreams of the city, the mandates and desires of God, and the calling and capacity of the church" (2004, 60). The role of transformational leaders involves responsibility that reaches far beyond the organizational leaders or churches. Service is not only a bridge to change, change is also the bridge to service. Together we can influence changes in individuals that will influence changes in the city by demonstrating the Gospel of Jesus Christ, a Christ-centered civic transformation.

Nehemiah's Burden

Collaboration for the purpose of community transformation is not easy to develop or maintain. The book of Nehemiah illustrates the difficulty in unifying a disparate group to transform a broken city. Nehemiah faced a bigger challenge than just building a wall to safeguard the city of Jerusalem. He had to draw "a contentious people of varied classes, cultures and dialects into a unified kinship. Unless this fractured group of Abraham's children could be pulled together as one community and rallied around a common vision, there would be little hope for the rebirth of their *Jeru-salem*—City of Peace" (Lupton, 2005, 29).

The transformative power of interdependence among believers can be seen here. The course of Nehemiah's life was changed by the information Hanani shared with him. Swanson and Williams showed that Nehemiah relied on Hanani to know the state of their people: "We should never underestimate the motivating and animating effect that good research plays in the lives of people. Recall the story of Nehemiah and how his life was changed when he asked his brother for two pieces of information: "Tell me about the city, and tell me about the people" (Neh 1:1–2). How Nehemiah acted upon this information to rebuild the city and the people of Jerusalem is told in the book of the Bible bearing his name.

The life of Nehemiah raises a challenging question: What am I willing to set aside to build the Kingdom of God? Nehemiah gave up a comfortable position as cupbearer to the king of Persia in order to lead a challenging reconstruction effort. He had to unite a large, disparate group: "From the names listed there are priests and Levites, administrative heads and merchants, and entire families, including daughters ... There is even listed a group of people who refused to have any part in the building project (Neh 3:5)" (Foster, 2005, 686)!

Nehemiah's life was changed when he understood the condition of the city of Jerusalem. "His burden to transform the city (Neh 1–7) and transform the people (Neh 8–13) came from accurate information" (Rusaw & Swanson, 2004, 158). Nehemiah conducted research both day and night that resulted in the deployment of resources for the work in Jerusalem. He is a great example of how the power of information can be used to change hearts and mobilize people to accomplish great things. As Rusaw and Swanson observed, this principle can be applied in the modern church: With statistical information and experience by the local churches, a joint strategy can be made to transform the city of Clovis. "To bear fruit, compassion must give birth to strategy" (Sider, Perkins, Gordon & Tizon, 2008, 159).

Nehemiah had great organizational and leadership skills but also great faith. He was a man of action and a man of prayer. Both action and prayer were needed to accomplish the work to which God called him: "He prayed for God's forgiveness, lamenting the grave sins of the people ... By praying this way, Nehemiah opened himself up to share the divine burden, to take on God's heart for the devastated poor, and to participate in what God wanted to do about the fallen city" (Sider, Perkins, Gordon & Tizon, 2008, 183).

Prayer is important for many reasons. For one, it binds hearts together and helps generate a united vision. As leaders come together and pray for their cities, praying together can be a great step toward working effectively together. Nehemiah led the people of Jerusalem forward in rebuilding not only the walls of Jerusalem but also the spiritual lives of the people.

Nehemiah presents a viable model for joining together to break down walls and make the city a safer and more desirable place to live and work. "Once Nehemiah was faced with the reality of the situation, there was kindled a fire in his bones. He could not but give himself—whatever the cost—to attempt the restoration of the city of God (see Neh 1:2–11)" (Dennison, 1999, 163).

A New Reality

Inside me is a deep and potent longing not for an idea but for an entirely new kind of reality, a reality where all the barriers and boundaries of separate entities are broken down.
Collaboration is a process that gets people to work together in new ways. The process does not end but spawns new collaborative ventures. Collaboration becomes a continuing phenomenon with a wide range of results that empower people and systems to change.

When people unite in trusting relationships they can build a strategy for community transformation, although forming a strategy is just the beginning. Dennison noted that "while solid relationships form the basis for unity, we can't stop there ... In order to complete our task in the city we must move beyond displays of unity and learn to walk in functional unity" (Dennison, 1999, 62). Functional unity is not about conformity or control. Dennison goes on to add that it is "a matter of uniting the Church around a common goal rather than around a cooperative project that would require each congregation to abandon its own ministries to participate in something external." It's an important distinctive.

Churches are just one of the players in city transformation. Of all the social and economic institutions in a city, churches and schools have the most sustaining permanence. One of the questions that Swanson & Williams pose in their book *To Transform a City* is, "What are the problems you most care about in your city?" While that is a good question to consider, there are more considerations. What problems does the city government see as the most urgent? The school leaders? Businesses? Nonprofit organizations? These authors remind us again, "We don't just work with people because they believe exactly as we do; we work with them because they care about the same things we care about in the city" (Swanson & Williams, 2008, 180).

It had only been a few years since I had moved to Clovis from out of state when I read that book. And being confronted with the question, "If your church no longer existed, would it be missed?" caused me to pause. Soon after that I contacted a city of Clovis administrative leader with inquiries on how our church could cooperate with them and other agencies in town. They presented numerous possibilities. They had previously contacted church leaders about cooperative opportunities but there had been little response. Now there had been major state budget cuts and their services to the community had been greatly reduced. To start with, the City expressed interest in having church members start after-school programs in low-income, high-crime apartment complexes, visitation programs for seniors in mobile home parks, and preemptive programs in "hot spot" areas.

This list was overwhelming at first for a church our size. I contacted people I knew from other churches and we put together teams to provide yard work and visitations at the mobile home parks, food distribution to the apartments and mobile home parks, and after-school programs in one of the apartments. The work started out strong but it wasn't easy to sustain.

Every project and every collaborative effort needs a champion, a person committed to both the vision and the process of partnership. A champion builds trust and grows confidence among group members. Champions work on relationship issues that come up. They lead in setting limited, achievable objectives. Champions develop consensus on one or two issues that would have the greatest impact if they were solved. They help groups recognize the progress they make along the way. Champions make the process as simple as possible without taking shortcuts (Butler, 2005, 201–205). Vision leaks and participants lose interest if someone is not regularly advocating for the purpose and the process of the alliance.

Champions initiate celebration, starting with the first small victory. Regular telephone calls and meeting with participants is crucial to maintain engagement. These contacts also encourage those involved to see how their contributions have furthered progress toward the vision of what can be if the alliance continues to work together. Champions spark the celebration of milestones reached.

Research and Education

With prayer and research, leaders can identify the assets within their organizations that can be deployed for city transformation. It is important to understand what God has been doing in and through people and in the city in order to know better what God now wants to accomplish. It takes constant networking with other churches and organizations to add to our teams.

As we saw in the story of Nehemiah, good research information can be helpful. Four years ago, statistics provided by the city of Clovis painted a different picture than most residents had. Drug, gang and other criminal activity is on the rise: arson, assault, theft, burglary, rape, robbery, even the murder rate, and this in a community with a polished image that prefers the pristine. When I interviewed local pastors, I often heard they were doing outreach in neighboring towns, but rarely in the community in which their church resides. Why? Because they were not informed of the needs, or what you might call opportunities. And as Jacob Huang pointed out in his chapter on "Using Data in Service of Community Transformation," good motivations are not enough either. Community data analysis is necessary so that the strategies can be made to meet unique characteristics of local residents.

Even people in other local towns have a perception of Clovis. While sharing all that I was discovering about the domestic violence cases and human trafficking as well as other crime, one man I was talking to responded emphatically, "Clovis? You don't have any issues in Clovis." Research is just the beginning, then the education must begin.

Dreaming about what can be as a result of mutual care and outreach is an important part of the process of making it happen. It starts with one person as the vision caster. As the process moves forward, more people can be invited into the envisioning phase; thus, more people will be involved in pushing the creative ends of what is possible. Stakeholders can dream together, sharing their individual hopes, and then work together to create a new future.

Inviting potential stakeholders to come together is not to convince them to be a part of a collaboration, but to collect information, build relationships, and seek positive consensus around the central questions of a need. Agreeing on a vision will require strong relationships and intentional communication among leaders in the community. Communication is vital in any relationship, and in partnerships that communication needs to be ongoing and conscious.

Samaria and Beyond (John 4:5–42)

God's people are called to love those who are different and perhaps marginalized by the world. There is no one who is a waste of the Christian's time or resources. Indeed, reaching those who are deemed worthless and even those regarded as hopelessly corrupt is the specific task of Christ's church.

In Jesus's time, Jewish people did not associate with Samaritans (John 4:9), but Jesus did. Jesus stopped and spoke to the lone woman in Samaria and healed her of the sins and hurts of her past. She told many others about the encounter and they came to believe in Jesus. In the meantime, Jesus said to his disciples:

> I tell you, open your eyes and look at the fields! They are ripe for harvest. Even now the reaper draws his wages, even now he harvests the crop for eternal life, so that the sower and the reaper may be glad together. Thus the saying 'One sows and another reaps' is true. I sent you to reap what you have not worked for. Others have done the hard work, and you have reaped the benefits of their labors (John 4:35b–38).

Not everyone is interested in working in the "Samaria" of Clovis. The southwestern part of the city is a tough area populated by the homeless, addicts, gangs, and all that results from such inhabitants. One of God's greatest desires is for people to be reconciled back to him;

Matthew 23:37b reminds us of Jesus' words: "How often would I have gathered your children together as a hen gathers her brood under her wings, and you were not willing!" As Rusaw and Swanson noted, "Sometimes as we focus on ourselves, our inadequacies, and our fears, we miss opportunities for ministry ... But if we are in ministry, we need to change our focus and realize it's not about us ... it's about them" (2004, 158). Community transformation is led by people who themselves are being transformed. This individual transformation occurs when a person submits to the lordship of Jesus Christ: "If anyone is in Christ, he is a new creation; the old has gone, the new has come" (2 Cor 5:17)! Walter Rauschenbusch expressed it well: "Personal rebirth and social rebirth are inseparably necessary. The social order cannot be saved without regenerate [people]" (Rusaw & Swanson, 2010, 48, gender specific language changed).

A proactive alliance of groups and organizations engaged in a project of mutual benefit can help develop and renew a sense of understanding, community, trust, and belonging. Together we can minister to and provide assistance to "the least of these." As "The King will reply, 'Truly I tell you, whatever you did for one of the least of these brothers and sisters of mine, you did for me'" (Matt 25:40).

With Open Hands

Spiritual writer Henri Nouwen explores how God can affect our lives when we choose to live with open hands. Open hands lead us to self-discovery, acceptance, hope, compassion, and revolution. All these are elements necessary for collaborative efforts. Nouwen wrote:

> You are Christian only so long as you look forward to a new world, so long as you constantly pose critical questions to the society you live in, so long as you emphasize the need of conversion both for yourself and for the world, so long as you in

no way let yourself become established in a situation of seeming calm, so long as you stay unsatisfied with the status quo and keep saying that a new world is yet to come. You are Christian only when you believe that you have a role to play in this new kingdom, and when you urge everyone you meet with holy unrest to make haste so that the promise might soon be fulfilled. So long as you live as a Christian you keep looking for a new order, a new structure, a new life. (1972, 126)

Engaging in an alliance with a clear goal in the city changes the way we work. We must move from competition to building consensus. Rather than working alone it includes working with a diverse set of cultures, fields, and/or sectors. The focus is on larger results and strategies instead of activities, services, and programs. While short-term accomplishments are good, the aim is long-term results. "We concentrate on what "we" want over and above what individual partners want. Listening to each other and thinking creatively become all-important" (Winer & Ray, 1996, 24).

City and Church Partnerships

Vision is the motivation of a healthy collaboration. Organizations with a common vision partner together for community transformation. Scripture has a lot to teach us about partnering with others. To have successful partnerships church leaders must acknowledge that God is the one who transforms and changes people's lives. God's ideal for his church is to be one (John 17:21). Phillip Butler reminds us, "From Genesis to Revelation, God's design seemed clear. Made in his image and based on Christ's transforming work in us, we're to live our lives in restored, open, trusting relationships that allow us to live and work *together*" (5).

We can easily become ineffective through a lack of clear vision. "Where there is no vision, the people perish" (Prov 29:18). Vision is deeply rooted in hope. That is the purpose of vision. As someone once said, vision gives pain a purpose. Without hope, we lose the endurance needed to see dreams realized. To affect change in the world around us, it comes down to the question of whether we want ownership or influence. Since the Kingdom of God within us is like leaven (1 Cor 5:6), we can permeate the world around us until we bring kingdom influence into every realm of society.

Senior leadership engagement is critical to collaboration success. There must be a strong commitment at the top level. In their book on urban ministry, Conn and Ortiz recognize, "Equipping the laity for urban ministry begins with the vision of the pastor and the leadership. The leadership of the church must have a commitment to mobilize the church for worship, the Word and mission to the world" (2001, 458–459).

As stated earlier, discernment of community needs is important in the process of ministry and in collaboration. There often is a difference between real and felt needs in society. "The felt needs of poor people often deal with the physical—food, housing, transportation, medicine. However, the deeper, real need has to do with valuing themselves as creations of God, reclaiming the dignity God desires them to have and finding the hope of a transformed life in Christ" (Conn & Ortiz, 2001, 291). Meeting this real need is what leads to changed lives. Collaborating with multiple sectors in a community can prompt holistic transformation.

Often, ministries address only felt needs, an approach that does not lead to transformed lives. Rusaw and Swanson claim that how people who minister view the community will affect the focus of ministry outreach (2004, 169). For community transformation, ministers have to view their cities through wide lenses. One church will have a limited view of the needs. Churches and other sectors of the community working together for transformation will have a much broader, more realistic understanding of the holistic needs. The goal of community transformation is not to meet just physical needs, but also spiritual and social needs. In collaboration, deeper needs can be met because "leaders have the ability to create something that doesn't exist...with resources they don't have" (2004, 216).

Followers of Jesus work in city administration and government, too, and they can be advocates for churches and ministries. Here are a number of examples of collaborative efforts between the city offices and faith-based organizations.

Care Fresno

A good model of collaboration is Care Fresno. Care Fresno was born in 1995 when the then-deputy chief of police Darrell Fifield came to many influential Christian leaders throughout Fresno and proposed, "If we (the police department) run the criminals out, will you (the church leaders) run the churches in?" High crime is often in highly-concentrated areas like apartment complexes. For years, the police would do a sweep of a complex and run out criminals, but within six months they were back, so the Police Chief was asking, "How do you maintain a complex once you get it cleaned up of the perpetrators?" They decided to go from a reactive response to a preventative one.

They realized that one of the keys was resident retention. If an apartment complex was a desirable environment for singles and families with no room for the criminals to return, this would help solve the problem. But if there were a lot of empty units, managers would be less discriminating of who they would rent to. This was when the Fresno police department, pastors, and local apartment complex owners, distressed by a high rate of crime calls from apartments, formed a collaborative partnership now called Care Fresno. The mission of Care Fresno was set to create safe and healthy communities throughout Fresno County in apartment complexes, community centers, and schools all brought about through the collaborative efforts of local police and sheriff's departments, faith-based organizations, and community agencies with resident input and leadership. Care Fresno has served thousands of children and adults in their programs since its inception through after-school tutoring, teaching English as a second language, job training, art classes, mentoring for at-risk youth, sports, carnivals, block parties, and much more.

In 1996, the prestigious Peter Drucker Foundation presented Care Fresno with the nationally-recognized Peter Drucker award for Nonprofit Innovation. In 2000, Care Fresno was one of the two Featured Programs that helped Fresno achieve the All-American City award.

Over the years, Care Fresno has adjusted their program as a result of the feedback they received from church leaders and volunteers. There is a greater emphasis on training church volunteers to better work with families who live in poverty and to better understand the cultural and class differences. This training has alleviated many of the frustrations due to misunderstandings and to move toward long-term, impactful steps the volunteers can take with the families. Curriculum and ministry plans have been further developed to address needs. Currently they have thirty young people living in twelve apartment complexes providing after-school tutoring and family-based services.

Clovis Police Department

The Clovis Police Department's motto is: "To provide superior protection and service in a manner that builds public confidence and improves the quality of life in our community. To those we serve, we want to be the best! Protection, Respect, Service, Quality, Teamwork, and Communication." Yet sometimes their efforts can result in an "us and them" mentality. Up until late 2014, the police department staff sponsored events in the community to build good will. Using the appropriated budget, they purchased items and put on a local event. While this was a service to some neighborhoods, it did not have an intentional community building emphasis.

In 2014, as a result of a Community Development Building Grant (CDBG) through the HUD–Housing & Urban Development government agency, Officer Kelly Orender was appointed to spearhead community events for the Police Department. Orender, a former social worker, enthusiastically embraced this new role since its focus was community outreach. Officer Orender began by inviting businesses, churches, local ministries and other individuals to get involved in sponsoring and participating in the events. The events drew hundreds of people and the numbers grew at each one. The police officers and firemen no longer just flip burgers and serve hot dogs; they are also playing sports with the kids. They bring out their trucks and rigs so the kids can climb on them and provide them with bike and helmet safety checks. A Blackhawk helicopter even made a landing at one of the events. Prayer booths are offered by local churches. City Chaplains serve nachos. Local businesses hand out produce and samples of their products. At the time of this writing, in particular, with mistrust between many police departments and communities across the country at the boiling point, these activities rise to the level of crucial.

One of the new events started in 2015 was COPS & KIDS. This was the first time officers donated their time to serve, play, and interact with school-aged kids. It was officer-driven in that several officers were appointed as leaders and they recruited their team members to lead different sports activities for a week during the summer. Numerous officers freely came out all week long as they felt this was a great way to give back to the community. The camp was marketed initially to lower-income and at-risk youth. Later it was decided to include any youth from the community. A local business donated t-shirts that were given to the volunteers and a local church sponsored the kids' t-shirts. Restaurants donated food for breakfasts and lunches. Volunteers from churches and other ministries came out and helped. Following the event, police officers commented they often run into kids in the community who were at the week-long camp.

Officer Orender has spent a lot of time building relationships with the police officers, local businesses, and the church leaders and volunteers. She regularly expressed her appreciation to all of them for their donations of time and other resources. Orender has seen the differences in the police officers as a result of engaging the community in this way as well as a great response from citizens. Bill Johnson mused, "Our thoughts become more shaped by the presence of evil around us than by the promise of God within us. Either we make an impact on the world around us, or it makes an impact on us" (2015, 17).

Collective Impact

The concept and proposal of Collective Impact made famous by Stanford has gained serious momentum nationally as a cross-sector approach to solving social (and environmental) problems. Collective impact is a newer model of collaboration among public, private, and nonprofit actors that emphasizes a common agenda, shared measurement systems, mutually reinforcing activities, continuous communication, and "backbone" support organizations. The Stanford

Social Innovation Review states, "Our research shows that successful collective impact initiatives typically have five conditions that together produce true alignment and lead to powerful results: a common agenda, shared measurement systems, mutually reinforcing activities, continuous communication, and backbone support organizations" (Hanleybrown, 2012).

In the collective impact model, community and church leaders, along with practitioners, come together around their desire to improve outcomes consistently over time. Collective impact is about advocating the practices you know get results in your own backyard. The focus is to spread the best of what exists here and now rather than the hope of future results. Collective impact can help fully grasp the shift that needs to be made to achieve population level impact. "Collective impact efforts are most effective when they build from what already exists; honoring current efforts and engaging established organizations, rather than creating an entirely new solution from scratch" (Hanleybrown et al, 2012).

The appeal of collective impact has many sources. The economic recession and the shortage of government funding has forced the social sector to find new ways to do more with less. Along these lines, disillusionment in the ability of governments to solve society's problems has caused people to look more closely at alternative models of change. The church has a greater opportunity to be part of the solution. We don't just work with people because they believe the way we do but rather we work with them because they care about the same things we care about in our community.

ENP's Approach to Collective Impact

Every Neighborhood Partnership (ENP) was formed only because of their collaborative vision. ENP doesn't really do ministry itself; instead they facilitate partnerships created through collaboration that results in outreach. ENP follows the collective impact model in that it gets multiple sectors to have a similar focus and share communication data, then facilitates ongoing work to address a felt need. Executive director Artie Padilla claims, "It's a multi sector approach because any felt need in a city is a complex issue and can only be addressed with as many of the sectors within a city as possible. All of our lives are intertwined with all of these sectors; most times we just don't realize it" (Padilla, personal communication, January 3, 2016).

ENP's role is to connect people from churches, universities and other organizations with opportunities to serve in the elementary schools and neighborhoods of our city. Imagine, connecting churches with over fifty of the ninety schools in a district in hands-on forms of assistance. The list of those with whom ENP collaborates with is extensive.

Lives are transformed as a result of this multi-sector collaboration with volunteers, students, and parents. Susan B. Anthony Elementary School is sandwiched between two of the poorest neighborhoods in Fresno, Lowell, and Webster. In the midst of a concentrated poverty neighborhood where crime is an issue, it hosts many transient families; this makes the school struggle with academic achievements.

Louisa was a student at Susan B. Anthony Elementary School from 2005-2012. She grew in her leadership abilities while part of the girls mentoring program her last two years at the school. She excelled in the classroom and was accepted to Edison Computech. She thrived there and now attends Edison High. Louisa is now the leader of Saturday sports at Susan B. Anthony Elementary and oversees the program with the church leaders and parents from the neighborhood. She is on the path toward medical school and is fluent in English and Spanish and is working on learning French.

Sandra lived across Susan B. Anthony Elementary when the ENP program was launched there in 2002. Her kids went to Saturday Sports and were hanging out in the neighborhood when various outreach projects were done. Sandra was married at the time. When the Neighborhood Thrift Store was launched in 2008, Sandra was the first volunteer. She came almost every day to help out, many times bringing her kids to help. A year later, Neighborhood Thrift moved to a larger building and Sandra became the first employee hired outside of management. At this time, she was a single mom. Sandra quickly grew in her ability to lead in the back warehouse and was promoted to warehouse manager in 2012. Late in 2014 she purchased her own home and continues to work at Neighborhood Thrift as warehouse manager.

Strategic Collaboration

Strategic collaboration does not happen instantaneously. It evolves through acts done together: "Growing confidence and partnership expertise lead to broader and more significant joint activities. Partnering fosters learning, which in turn facilitates cooperation with other partners, thereby generating a collaboration multiplier effect" (Austin, 2000, 86). Envisioning the future together, especially after fruitful collaborative projects, can attract the involvement of others. Some people stand on the sidelines watching, and they may join in when they see successful outcomes. The more partners involved, the greater the opportunities for synergistic activity and good outcomes for Christ-centered civic transformation.

One reason the church exists is to foster change and transformation in the world around us. Bill Johnson noted that, "The impact of the Church on the value system of our cities has been strong at some times, and seemingly nonexistent at other times" (2015, 13).

Role of Media

We should emphasize the role of the media in helping make connections for us. As shared in the beginning of this chapter, our church got connected to the Food Pantry Coalition after I had read about it in *The Fresno Bee*. Sam Williams shared the story about his church opening the Gilead House in Novato, CA and the local newspaper covered the celebration story with a full article including photos. The next day a woman called and offered to donate another house if the church would open an additional place where women and children could live and be cared for in a full array of services. Through this partnership, this woman started attending church, had a life-changing encounter with Jesus, and eventually became the future director of the program (2010, 177).

After we had been involved in the Food Pantry Coalition in Clovis for a couple of years, a reporter called the local newspaper asking for an interview on our church's participation. This launched a series of articles she wrote over the year on various collaborative efforts and also started a great friendship. A desire we shared is that members of the media are shaped by personal integrity and driven by a value for the truth. Our desire is to further transform relationships between the church and other sectors of the community to move from skepticism to trust. Therefore, fostering relationships of trust with the media is crucial.

Kingdom experiences and values are transferable to every part of society. Collaboration is countercultural. Yet, "Few people will disagree with the principles; the difficulty is in knowing how to turn them into action. To do that, we have to learn from one another with humility" (Davis, 2015, 213). The body of Christ is called to be a countercultural force in our communities. Jesus himself was the most countercultural of all. Just read his Sermon on the Mount. It is truly a solution for a broken world.

Other Informal Partners

My phone rang and when I went to answer it, I didn't recognize the local number. The gentleman calling was a member of a car club in town. They had over 300 members and decided at one of their meetings they wanted to do a food drive to benefit their community. So they called the city asking for a good source that would distribute the food to people in need. They were given my number. Not only did they do a food drive among their club members and at the dealership, they placed nine barrels at businesses in Old Town Clovis for community members to fill. At the end of the food drive, they had a car show downtown and filled another pickup load of food for our food distribution. When I went down to the car show to meet some of the club members, I was able to share with them where we distribute the food and educate them on some of the needier parts of town. They asked how they could help more.

Another call came from a local Christian motorcycle club looking for opportunities to serve the community. Timing and passion collided when a member of the Christian Motorcyclists Association (CMA) responded to a call on his heart to expand the local Fresno chapter of CMA into a new Clovis chapter. At a state rally in May 2013, the Sword and Shield Riders (SSR) were birthed as an established Clovis ministry.

CMA has a solid biblical foundation and core values of prayer, fellowship, discipleship and evangelism. When God calls for his hands and feet, Clovis SSR is willing to minister in service to the community at neighborhood events or biker rallies, praying over the riders and blessing them and their bikes. Riding motorcycles is just a bonus. Their first passion is watching God open doors and bring people together to hear about Jesus.

Regularly our church receives a call from someone who was given our phone number from a Clovis city leader. We repeatedly contacted the city administration to express our desire to serve our greater community. After several months, they called us with a need in the community. Members from our church responded right away and took care of it. Then we received another call. A leader from the city invited us to their offices for a meeting to discuss how we could work more closely together. This has been a great value from building the relationship with the city directors. The calls have become more frequent and our church has gotten more churches involved in meeting these needs. The City has come to value the partnership with local churches.

How We Are Overcoming Barriers

Three main obstacles for collaboration found among churches in Clovis are time limitations, shortage of staff, and communication of opportunities (Lawler, 2012, 103). A podcast by Stew (Michael Stewart) of Verge Network, entitled *Seven habits of highly effective difference-makers* (vergenetwork.org), surveyed 5000 missional leaders and discovered the two top obstacles to being a difference maker are knowing where and how to start and making time. Time and communication of opportunities are common barriers.

Branson and Martinez explain why overcoming obstacles is so important. "Because the church is to participate in the life and activities of God, we believe our work is to discern ways we are to actively enter into God's initiatives in the world" (2011, 44). Transformation through collaboration happens when the church grows to care about the people God cares about and begins working where he is at work. "Developing and sustaining effective partnerships takes great prayer, vision, energy, long-term commitment, and patience" (Butler, 2005, 204).

Communication is a challenge in any partnership: marriage, business, friendship, church. James Austin, a professor of business at Harvard University Graduate School, writes, "Good communication is essential to building trust, and trust is the intangible that makes a collaboration cohesive" (2000, 180). Building trust and mutual respect takes time and effort; it doesn't happen in one meeting or conversation. Communication must be open, regular, and meaningful. Collaboration requires communication that is clear and inclusive, and that shares information among all the stakeholders.

Discovery of where and how is an essential component in collaboration, and it is most fruitful when done in community. Discovery is the beginning of meaningful collaboration. Phillip Butler called the discovery stage "exploration" and described how it works: "You'll be asking questions and listening, expanding your personal base of information, and multiplying relationships. You'll also be broadening your understanding about the realities of the vision you have in mind and the perceptions of others" (2005, 121). There is a need to continue asking questions and making sure you are in touch with the people you are committed to reaching and serving with Jesus's love and power. In discovery, leaders come together to listen to one another, learn from one another, pray together, and discover the way forward to be transformational change agents in the community.

The Body of Christ

In Revelation 5, John shares his vision of what the throne scene of the global body of Christ will be one day. People from every tribe, language, people, and nation will be gathered together as one kingdom and priests to serve and worship God. In his refreshing new look on missional principles, Charles Davis claims, "When it comes to the body of Christ, *better* is defined as love and unity between vastly different human beings, male and female, rich and poor, Jew and Gentile, together as one body—truly the only solution for a broken planet" (2015, 212).

Bill Hybels has been quoted to say, "The hope of the world is the local church." Davis takes this one step further: "The body of Christ with Jesus as Lord—not playing church—is indeed, the best hope for the world" (2015, 216).

When a variety of entities in a community work together, they can change the face of society. One day, when Jesus inaugurates his visible reign over all the earth, people from every culture who have followed Him will "be a kingdom and priests to serve our God, and they will reign on the earth" (Rev 5:10).

Next Generation Collaboration

In closing, I want to share something tremendous I see happening before my eyes – next generation collaborative leadership taking shape. It also illustrates that in order to effectively participate in the social and spiritual transformation of the community, continuous personal transformation must take place. The Clovis Police Department sponsored a neighbor event in one of the low-income, high-risk pockets of the community. Offering hamburgers, hot dogs, cotton candy, ice cream, and other snacks, they were also there to pass out backpacks with school supplies to the kids. As a chaplain for the police department, I was working the nacho machine.

Three Hispanic young men walked through the food line. I assumed they were part of the neighborhood. I grabbed my own hot dog and went to eat with them. As it turns out, these young men did not live in the area but were there to volunteer by engaging the youth in games. Anthony shared his personal story. Anthony had made some bad choices as a teenager and entered the Marine Corps to try to solve these problems. Unfortunately, he didn't give up drinking or smoking illegal substances. He eventually got kicked out of the Marine Corps due to testing positive in a drug test.

After returning home, he was depressed and hopeless and lived, in his own words, a very selfish life. He started breaking and entering vehicles to steal personal items to fund his next high. Eventually he was caught and thrown into jail for a hundred days. When he was released, his cousin invited him to Celebration Church. Philippians 3:13, "Forget about those things which are behind and reach, move, strain and press forward to what lies ahead," spoke loudly to him. He was healed mentally, emotionally, and spiritually and finally felt hope in his life. Anthony was able to get his AA degree and then entered the Celebration School of Leadership.

The School of Leadership run by the church encourages community outreach through partnership with local businesses and organizations. The Clovis Boys and Girls Club was hosting the Back to the School event in partnership with the City of Clovis Police Department. Anthony and a few of his fellow students continually look for such volunteer opportunities and are there to help impact the next generation.

He plans to become a counselor and help youth discover a brighter future for their lives, too. In his two years of education and experience, Anthony believes "we can make an impact and transform our communities by all of us not doing everything, but all doing something."

As H. Spees proclaims, "Jesus has made us one in John 17. Now the challenge for us is to *operationalize* the unity of the body of Christ for the transformation of our city."

Works Cited

Austin, J. E. (2000). The Collaboration Challenge: How Nonprofits and Businesses Succeed through Strategic Alliances, 1st ed., Drucker Foundation Future Series. San Francisco: Jossey-Bass.

Barth Jr., G. (2010). *The Good City: Transformed Lives Transforming Communities.* Tallmadge, OH: S.D. Myers Publishing Services.

Branson, M.L. and Martinez, J.F. (2011). Churches, Cultures and Leadership: A Practical Theology of Congregations and Ethnicities. Downers Grove, IL: IVP Academic.

Butler, P. (2005). *Well Connected: Releasing Power and Restoring Hope through Kingdom Partnerships.* Waynesboro, GA: Authentic Media.

Conn, H. and Ortiz M. (2001). *Urban Ministry: The Kingdom, the City, and the People of God.* Downers Grove, IL: InterVarsity Press.

Crutchfield, L. and Grant, H. (2008). *Forces for Good.* San Francisco: Jossey-Bass.

Davis, C.A. (2015). Making Disciples Across Cultures: Missional principles for a diverse world. Downers Grove, IL: InterVarsity Press.

Dennison, J. (1999). City Reaching: On the road to community transformation. Pasadena: William Carey Library.

Foster, R.J. (2005) *The Renovaré Spiritual Formation Bible: New Revised Standard Version with Deuterocanonical Books, 1st ed.* San Francisco: Harper.

Halter H. and Smay M. (2010) *And: The Gathered and Scattered Church*, Exponential Series Grand Rapids, MI: Zondervan.

Hanleybrown, F, Kania, J., and Kramer, M. (2012). Channeling Change: Making Collective Impact Work. *Stanford Social Innovation Review.*

Johnson, B. (2015). *The Power that Changes the World*. Bloomington, MN: Chosen Books.

Lawler, C.S. (2012). Church Collaboration for City Transformation in a Context of Affluence. D.Min dissertation. Bakke Graduate University, Seattle.

Lawson-Swezey, C. (2014, January 16) Unique program helps feed city's hungry. Clovis Roundup, p. 1.

Lupton, R. D. (2005). *Renewing the City: Reflections on Community Development and Urban Renewal* Downers Grove, IL: InterVarsity Press.

Nouwen, H. (1972). *With Open Hands*. Notre Dame: Ave Maria Press.

Roschelle, J., and S. Teasley. (1995). The construction of shared knowledge in collaborative problem solving. In Computer supported collaborative learning, ed. C. E. O'Malley, 69–97. Heidelberg: Springer-Verlag.

Rusaw, R. and Swanson E. (2004). *The Externally Focused Church*. Loveland, CO: Group Publishing.

Sider, R.J., Perkins, J. M., Gordon, W.L. & Tizon, F.A. (2008). *Linking Arms, Linking Lives: how urban-suburban partnerships can transform communities*. Grand Rapids, MI: Baker Books.

Swanson, E. and Williams S. (2010). To Transform a City: *Whole Church, Whole Gospel, Whole City*. Grand Rapids, MI: Zondervan.

Winer, M. & Ray, K. (1996). *Collaboration Handbook: Creating, Sustaining, and Enjoying the Journey*. Saint Paul, MN: Amherst H. Wilder Foundation.

Chapter Five

The Power of a Youth-Led Faith and Justice Ministry

Yammilette Rodriquez

Youth Leadership Institute and United Faith Christian Fellowship

"I speak not for myself but for those without voice… those who have fought for their rights… their right to live in peace, their right to be treated with dignity, their right to equality of opportunity, their right to be educated."

Malala Yousafzai

My husband Jim and I are volunteer, bi-vocational senior pastors at United Faith Christian Fellowship (UFCF), a Mennonite Brethren congregation located in the heart of Southeast Fresno. We attended UFCF since 1999 as recent college graduates, Jim taking the role of treasurer and serving on the board, I serving as the youth director and singing on the worship team. In 2008, we were appointed associate pastors and worked alongside the senior pastors. Under their leadership we shared the same passion to love UFCF and the community that surrounded it. The church was built in the 1940s as a Quaker ministry and the neighborhood rose up around it. Even then, the purpose of the church was to be truly present in the neighborhood.

In the summer of 2011, the senior pastors of our church left unexpectedly and moved their family to another state. At that point, we were next in line in leadership; we were asked if we would be willing to take the role. This was a difficult and prayerful decision. Our first child was born in January of 2011, Jim worked for the Mennonite Central Committee as their chief financial officer and traveled around the world conducting audits, and I was two years in my job as a full-time director for a local youth organization. Needless to say, we had an incredibly full plate, not to mention all of the community boards and committees we served on. I would have imagined that any couple in this circumstance would have rejected the offer to volunteer. However, we felt the Holy Spirit tugging and guiding us to love this community and to do it at a greater capacity; to help guide the direction of the church to truly live in community with its neighbors and address the issues of poverty and oppression hand-in-hand. In August of 2011, we were named senior pastors.

I have been a youth director in the church setting since I was 18 years old and have continued to do youth work at my local church until today. In many churches I have encountered, there is the stated belief that "Jesus is all they need," but I have always struggled with that. I grew up in a church where that was the mentality, but yet outside the church door there was extreme poverty, violence, and substance abuse. How could someone even think of "accepting Jesus" when they were worried about where the next meal was going to come from or fearful of walking outside their door? Jesus is definitely our foundation, but we as urban youth workers also need to provide walls and roof to support the growth of a young person (Clark & Powell, year, 91). I am now an activist and minister in an urban community, and my life's mission is to create space for more love and compassion to unite our communities. Youth leadership is essential in this process. We have seen the ways that hate and fear only divide us more and cause chaos and turmoil. As Dr. King so famously said, "Injustice anywhere is a threat to justice everywhere." I believe that if we had more ways to carry out love, reconciliation, compassion, and forgiveness, there would be less brokenness in this world. A lack of love is at the root of so many negative issues in our cities. We are discovering how youth are the creative conveyers of that love.

Youth are the Present, Not Just the Future

So what role do youth play in addressing this lack of justice, this lack of love? Youth factor prominently into the way our church sees mission. We are a neighborhood church that serves its surrounding community. We are committed to serving those in need and practicing faith in action. Some examples of UFCF ministries that help the underserved include a food ministry, a career development/professional ministry aimed to help underserved women, and a community garden and a youth/young adult ministry that works to advocate for positive changes in the community. Since we took on the pastorship, we have moved into a more action-based ministry to dig deeper into what it meant to have a methodology of practicing faith and justice in a manner that used the youth and developed leadership in the process. It required our church to assess if our ministries were shallow or producing deep change. If we believed, as we said we did, that our mission was to "love justice, show mercy and walk humbly before God" (Mic 6:8), then the whole church, including our youth, needed to have ways to live that out. We would have to train and empower our youth to live justly. The act of loving justice is also to empower others to know how to live justice. As a youth advocate in my day job I find this is central to my mission. Through our church youth-led advocacy work, UFCF is on this journey to create opportunities for young people to be a part of true sustainable change in their communities. Practicing faith and justice means to go beyond simply having food and clothing giveaways on Saturdays to exploring and addressing the core issues and root causes of poverty in our community. UFCF's advocacy work is an effort to involve youth and young adults in partnership to create healthy communities. We see it as a roadmap to change, in which the youth work must always align with the Cross. Change can't happen without God in the midst of it.

Responding to Violence, A Pivot Toward Justice

In 2012, our church congregation experienced an act of violence in our church neighborhood. A church congregant's home was subject to a drive-by shooting. It was a terrifying and horrifying experience for the family and the church community. It was the week of Halloween and our church was grieving and frustrated with the violence in our neighborhood. We organized a press conference that week in front of the church bringing together neighboring churches, CBOs, city elected officials, K-12 and higher education representatives, and the police chief. The message was, "Enough is enough." Our local television news covered the press conference and interviewed our sister whose home had been in the crossfire. She said, "My parents' home was struck four times, two of which hit the wall of my parents' bedroom, and my mom hasn't been able to sleep since it occurred. What can my mom do? My father doesn't know what to do. Can he protect his family?" Hearing this created a yearning desire for justice in the hearts of our younger congregants, motivating them to take action and learn how to create positive change.

This violent event in our community catalyzed the formation of a group of youth leaders who call themselves The South East Neighborhood Transformation Team (SENTT). The faith and justice perspective is the core of the SENTT Team. The purpose and mission of the youth leaders is "United to empower the voice of the community through their lens, with a Christ-centered youth perspective that leads to sustainable transformation." So focused has this group of youth become on the pursuit of justice in the name of Jesus that since 2012, SENTT has partnered with elected officials to create policy that will help to reduce violence and ensure sustainable change that will benefit generations. This project involved our youth conducting a review of all liquor stores in our neighborhood (vastly greater than the number allowed by state law), assessing the window ads and the floor-level advertising for alcohol and cigarettes (because these influence children), reviewing the levels of nutritious food available, and more, and then working with local officials to shape an ordinance that will establish healthier practices. I will describe this particular project in detail later in this chapter. But first it is important to understand the backdrop of partnership that needed to exist for our youth to have that kind of impact. The SENTT Team is carrying out the desire of creating a deeper justice mission for the use of our church and young adult ministry, but they aren't doing it alone.

Collective Impact for the Betterment of our Community Through Secular and Faith-based Partnerships

My role as Senior Director for Youth Leadership Institute (YLI) is to help young people and their adult allies come together to create positive social change. YLI values the role of the faith-based organizations in the community and knows that building healthier communities cannot happen if core partners are not at the table. Since YLI is intentional about including faith-based organizations and/or churches in community change work, the work of SENTT has truly been a model of *Collective Impact* for creating systems change in Fresno. Collective Impact brings people together in a structured way to achieve social change. It starts with a common agenda and strong communication and fosters mutually reinforcing activities. With the connection that I have with United Faith Christian Fellowship and YLI, the partnership of both entities is powerful. In addition to these two initial strong partners, SENTT has been intentional in bringing others to the table, such as the Fresno County Public Health Department, local city Council members, community leaders, other CBOs, law enforcement, and other churches.

The Process of True Youth Development

Decades of research have confirmed the central components of a positive Youth Development Framework, and we root our activities in that framework. Young people need a safe environment, opportunity to build skills, experiences developing positive peer and adult relationships, and meaningful and authentic opportunities to demonstrate leadership and contribute to their community through active engagement and involvement, and these standards need to be infused in all experiences young people have at a community level. Over the years, we have expanded to include churches and faith-based communities, and SENTT is one of the projects that has a Christ-centered focus.

Positive Youth Engagement is a concept in which youth are seen as community resources and assets. Youth are engaged to explore and develop solutions and partner with community and other stakeholders to create positive change. Authentic engagement of young people requires a shift in mindset and sharing of power regarding how decisions are made in communities and in institutions. Youth engagement is critical to long-term community change. The eight principles of youth engagement have three core strengths—capacity, motivation, and opportunity—and all of them lay a foundation for young people to be actively engaged in social change efforts. According to Pittman and Martin, organizations that seek to engage youth need a strong foundation and a stable operational infrastructure that is suited to the level and type of youth engagement desired (Pittman and Martin, 2007, 11). Youth engagement can only truly be effective once the foundation is solid with the first two principles: strong outreach strategies and a strong home base which is defined as an organizational resource and adult support system. Only after the foundation is clearly laid out can the other six principles come into play for intentional and true youth engagement. Those are as follows:

a. Convey an intentional philosophy
b. Identify core issues
c. Create youth and adult teams
d. Build youth and adult capacity
e. Provide individual supports
f. Sustain access and influence

How This Works for Us

These concepts truly develop the whole person and value young people as resources. This philosophy helps grow local leadership, foster long-term, sustainable youth and community engagement and mobilization, and build social movements that include youth leaders who are most impacted by community problems. For the past few years, our church has ingrained these principles in our youth leaders. Culture change is sometimes difficult in youth ministry, thus we have been very intentional about instilling these practices in our work with adult allies and youth to ensure that youth are valued and seen as leaders and resources. Our adult allies have been trained in youth development principles with the goal of evolving from an activity-based youth ministry to an action-based ministry. The action-based methods began with SENTT regularly gathering at their neighborhood church to talk about the changes they wanted to see in their neighborhood. Youth leaders were key decision-makers in the process of determining this project. YLI partnered with youth to build their capacity to make the changes they want to see in their neighborhood. We helped develop the skills and knowledge of SENTT youth and their adult allies to advocate for alcohol outlets to stop inundating their community with unhealthy advertisements. We also helped strengthen the collaboration, trust, and relationships between youth and adult allies to foster an effective and productive youth and adult team. We conducted trainings that built skills in advocacy and organizing, action research, leadership, youth and adult partnerships, team work, and environmental prevention strategies for community change as well as present opportunities for intentional trust and relationship building between youth members of SENTT and their adult allies through structured team-building activities.

Through our many years of partnering with youth and communities, we are demonstrating that through building the leadership skills and knowledge of local youth and adults to advocate for healthy changes in their communities, it is possible to create a network of empowered youth and adults equipped to address social justice issues that arise in the neighborhood, thus improving the quality of life for all residents living in the southeast Fresno community. Likewise, if SENTT youth and their adult allies are successful in their efforts, liquor stores in the southeast Fresno neighborhood will display significantly fewer unhealthy ads, thereby improving the overall health of the community. The long-term strategy for sustainability is to build the capacity of the community residents and youth to sustainably address any and all social justice issues that arise in their communities beyond the scope of this project.

Youth Development Standards of Practice

An extensive body of research illustrates that youth development is an effective approach to preventing problems and increasing positive outcomes for youth. These outcomes include areas such as building social and personal skills. The standards were developed to represent a set of critical supports, opportunities, and skills that young people need to experience on a consistent basis to foster and sustain personal and social competencies and to achieve long-term developmental outcomes that promote youth as productive members of society (Commission on Positive Youth Development, 2005; Connell, Gambone and Smith, 1998; Werner and Smith, 1982; Tierney, Grossman and Resch, 1995; and Benard, 1991). According to the five standards of practice, young people have experienced the following through their involvement with our programs:

A Safe Environment

· Physical Safety

· Emotional Safety

Opportunities for Community Engagement

· Knowledge of Community

· Interaction / Interface with the Community

· Communication with the Community

· Contribution to the Community

Opportunities for Leadership and Advocacy

· Decision-Making and Governance

· Youth Voice

· Action

Opportunities to Build Caring and Meaningful Relationships with Peers and Adults

· Peer Knowledge
· Adult Knowledge / Guidance
· Emotional Support
· Practical Support
· Sense of Belonging

Opportunities to Engage in Interesting and Relevant Skill Development Activities

· Specific Skills
· Challenging and Interesting Activities

These standards of practice are based on three distinct—but complementary—evidence-based frameworks for understanding youth development: McLaughlin (2000), Eccles & Gootman (2002), and Gambone, Klem & Connell (2002). Each of these frameworks is based on a review of multiple longitudinal studies of youth programs and settings and the outcomes that youth achieved through their engagement in these settings. In the following table, we highlight the key elements of each framework:

Table 1

Study	Key Findings and Components
Community Counts: How Youth Organizations Matter for Youth Development	Positive Development Outcomes: • Academic Success • Self-Confidence and Optimism • Civic Responsibility • Paths to Success Necessary Community Supports: • Leadership & Passion • Community Contexts • Community 'Menu' • Diverse Expertise • Listening to Youth • Support for Core Activities • Making Youth a Line Item • Meaningful Measures of Accomplishment • Youth-Based Resources • Community Youth Development McLaughlin, M. (2000).
Community Programs to Promote Youth Development	Positive Developmental Outcomes: • Physical Development (for example, health knowledge and behavior) • Intellectual Development (for example, skills and academic performance) • Psychological and Emotional Development (for example, ability to cope, plan) • Social Development (for example, sense of

	connectedness, civic participation) Necessary Supports and Opportunities: • Physical and Psychological Safety • Appropriate Structure • Supportive Relationships • Opportunities to Belong • Positive Social Norms • Support for Efficacy and Mattering • Opportunities for Skill Building • Integration of Family, School and Community Efforts Eccles, J. & Gootman, J.A. (Eds.), (2002).
Finding Out What Matters for Youth: Testing Key Links in a Community Action Framework for Youth Development	Establishes link between experiencing supports and opportunities and long-term positive outcomes for young people • Youth with positive outcomes on developmental milestones in high school are more likely to have good outcomes in their early twenties and • Conversely, youth with poor developmental outcomes in high school are more likely to have poor outcomes in early twenties Gambone, M.A., Klem, A.M. & Connell, J.P. (2002).

It Works

In other words, research indicates that when these key features are incorporated into a youth program or setting, youth will experience the supports and opportunities necessary to foster positive developmental outcomes, which ultimately leads to longer-term positive outcomes such as economic self-sufficiency, responsibility, and civic participation (Eccles & Gootman, 2002).

Since a strong body of scientific evidence has established that applying a youth development framework in a setting leads to positive short- and long-term youth development outcomes and prevents problems, the focus of program assessment and evaluation shifts away from participant outcomes and centers on the question of whether the program is providing young people with this set of key supports and opportunities.

Table 2

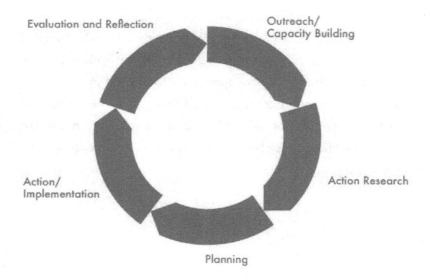

The Project: Youth-Driven Alcohol Outlet Density Study

Through critically examining their communities, youth noticed an abundance of liquor outlets with numerous alcohol, tobacco, and junk food advertisements covering the windows. Upon researching the issue, youth discovered that alcohol outlet density is a key determinant in the amount of alcohol advertising in a community. Merchants use storefronts and the interiors of alcohol outlets to advertise alcohol products. Therefore, areas with a high density of outlets have a greater number of advertisements. There is also ample evidence from a variety of studies demonstrating that the degree of youth alcohol advertising exposure is strongly and directly associated with intentions to drink, age of drinking onset, prevalence of drinking, and the amount consumed (American Association of Pediatrics, 1999, 341–343). Furthermore, several studies have found that in and near neighborhoods where there is a high density of places that sell alcohol, there is a higher rate of violence (Gruenewald, P.J. and Remer, L., 2004, 1084).

The southeast neighborhood is in the 93702 zip code and has a population of nearly 50,000, 75% of which is Latino. Studies have found there are five times more alcohol advertisements in Latino neighborhoods than in predominantly white neighborhoods (Alaniz, M.L. and Wilkes, C., 1995, 430–51). The community has some of the highest concentrated poverty in Fresno County with a median household income of 27,372 and 45% of families living at or below the federal poverty line (2009-2013 American Community Survey 5-Year Estimates). With a median age of 24, nearly 60% of residents are under the age of 30. In 93702, 50%of the population is male and 50% is female (factfinder.census.gov, Nov. 2015).

PhotoVoice Project Provided Foundation

That process of launching the project started with a PhotoVoice project in the summer of 2012 that enabled youth to express what they saw in their community. PhotoVoice is an assessment method which combines photography and social action. We integrated the PhotoVoice assessment method with our youth development model to ensure youth were equipped with the knowledge and skills necessary to lead the project. The youth began the project through assessing their neighborhood through community mapping to determine issues in the 93702 zip code, one of the most impoverished areas in Fresno. Analyzing the results of the assessments, the youth decided to target the issue of liquor outlet saturation in impoverished communities and are currently aiming towards making positive community and policy change to

improve Fresno (see attached 2012 PhotoVoice photos in Appendix A).
Youth worked with local corner store owners to have them sign a pledge
to be more family-friendly stores. Our youth walked the community
together to acknowledge the assets present in the community. There were
so many resources that stood out that we hadn't noticed before (see map
in Appendix B). The neighborhood of the church includes schools,
diverse churches, community gardens, cooling centers, trees, numerous
small business owners, a bank, and diverse restaurants. When they
conducted a PhotoVoice assessment and went deeper to discover the
story of the UFCF community they found...

Space: A diverse community with more than 100 languages spoken in
Fresno; during elections households have signs; two blocks away there
are historical homes over 100 years old; there are empty lots with so
much potential

Structures: Our church is a perfect example of the structure of homes in
the area, custom-made with so much character; we are very far away
from the "tract home look."

Scraps of Life: A local homeowner decided to be the example in recycling
and created her own trashcans in front of her home so passersby can
deposit their recyclables .

Signage: There has been unsanctioned graffiti on numerous occasions on
our church and on store walls.

Sounds and Smells: The youth always hear cultural music; birds chirping
and the game coming from TV sets; so many languages spoken from

households; people mowing their lawns; the horn of the elote (corn) man and the ice cream truck; sounds of house fans and swamp coolers; cars passing and sometimes police helicopters and sirens. The neighborhood has scents from the taco shop and other cultural foods.

Signs of Hope: There are numerous churches; there are nonprofit organizations, local schools, and healthcare providers.

Social Interactions: The youth noticed churches that conduct neighbor activities; entrepreneurial spirit in the community of people selling corn, churros, duros, nieve (ice cream) and tamales and having yard sales; local corner stores who have relationships with customers. There are many little children and elderly. There is a lot of gang life around our community.

One thing that stood out to the SENTT youth was that although our neighborhood is an impoverished area, there are so many members of the neighborhood that have the entrepreneurial spirit to make ends meet. The sense of family is everywhere with families gathered for dinner, playing outside or just sitting on their porches. Through the process of the storeowner pledges we now know them by name and live in community. The youth were pleasantly surprised that a few more speed limit signs have come up. There are still so many empty lots but there is potential there for growth.

The Model Spreads: Youth Influence Youth

Now every spring break, in partnership with YLI, our youth train other church youth to be advocates in areas and teach them how to conduct a PhotoVoice, do community mobilization, work on policy and social change, and work with elected officials and they spend their spring break advocating with local elected officials and proposing local legislation to help address the issue in their neighborhoods such as liquor outlet saturation, negative and unhealthy advertising, and the prevalence of violence.

SENTT has worked on a resource map they used as a tool to give to local community members and share with decision-makers. It is very important for this process to be a true youth and adult partnership; therefore SENTT ranges from people 13-40 years old. The neighborhood also has an oversaturation of liquor stores that display numerous unhealthy advertisements for alcohol, tobacco, e-cigarettes, and junk food, many of those ads directly targeting youth and children. In 2014, SENTT youth mapped the concentration of liquor stores around Roosevelt High School, the only high school in 93702, and found there are 35 liquor outlets within a one-mile radius. One of our young adult leaders, Janet Salcedo, a SENTT Adult Ally and Fresno Pacific University student, was recently asked to speak before hundreds of community leaders. She stated, "We cannot allow the alcohol industry to continue to target youth and underserved communities at the cost of our community's health."

The youth had their first Town Hall meeting in the summer of 2014 and created an asset map to share with neighborhood residents, community members, and elected officials. They have had an annual Town Hall meeting since then to get authentic community input and be a bridge to the decision makers of Fresno.

The Fresno Bee

HOME | NEWS | SPORTS | FRESNO STATE BULLDOGS | BUSINESS | LIVING & ENTERTAINMENT | OPINION | LOCAL DEALS | dealsaver

News > Local News

Southeast Fresno neighborhood group gets update on liquor store limits

BY BRIANNA VACCARI
The Fresno Bee August 12, 2014

More than a dozen youths and adults who have worked for two years to crack down on the abundance of liquor stores in southeast Fresno got some good news Tuesday night: They finally have the ear of someone who can help.

The Cross-Generational Neighborhood Transformation Team, a collaboration of a church's Friday Night Live youth program and the Youth Leadership Institute, has been meeting with community leaders and urging liquor stores to cut back on alcohol and tobacco advertising in store windows in the neighborhood around United Faith Christian Fellowship Church, near Cedar and Belmont avenues.

The group hosted a town hall meeting at the church Tuesday evening, where about 80 people heard Gregory Barfield, Council Member Oliver Baines' chief of staff, say that Baines is trying to update a city ordinance governing liquor stores.

Barfield said the update would tighten city restrictions on alcohol and tobacco signs in store windows.

Fresno County's Public Health Department found 40% of Fresno liquor stores violate state laws limiting signs on store windows, restrictions that are intended to aid law enforcement.

The Friday Night Live youth met with Baines during the students' spring break to voice their concerns.

"Community change does not happen overnight," said Yammilette Rodriguez, the Youth Leadership Institute's program director. "We can't make change alone."

RECENT HEADLINES

Wildfire destroys at least 10 homes near Bass Lake, prompts wide evacuations
14 minutes ago

Yosemite's Meadow fire estimated cost at $3.9 million to date

21st Congressional District: Valadao, Renteria differences murky

Dan Walters: Taxes on rich closed the state

Throughout these past three years, the SENTT Team has been asked to give presentations or training on the advocacy work, and they noticed that language of extreme needs and problems was a way we communicated the reasoning behind the work. Yet when people from other places in Fresno talked down on the 93702 community the youth felt a sense of regret that they used the negative language. Since then, SENTT has changed their verbiage to reflect the love for the UFCF church community and lift up the many assets of southeast Fresno. We need to ask our community members the same question Jesus asked: "What do you want me to do for you?" We know that sin has increased in our communities and I myself find cling to Romans 5:20: where sin increased, grace abounded all the more. SENTT's goal is not to decide what is good for the neighborhood but to engage them and ask them directly.

How Systems Thinking Impacted the UFCF Ministry

Through partnership with YLI the youth and young adults have been trained to know how to mobilize communities and how to have a systemic response to the issues. The SENTT adult allies have then taught church members how to do community mobilization with the lens of Christ. *The Washington Post* reported that, according to the Brookings Institution, ten years ago Fresno was known as number one in concentrated poverty in the state, pollution, gang activity, and many other issues, but we can no longer stay in the realm of the physical or relational response. It is very easy for the church to stay in that form of ministry because it is tangible. You can see the relief in families' eyes when you hand them food or give them clothing. But how much more of a difference can the church make when we deal with the core problems of poverty in our communities, when we look beyond the band-aid solutions and look to impact people on a greater scale? What an impact the can church have when we fix systems involved in the process and influence decision makers to make changes for the future. UFCF has reshaped their youth/young adult ministry to consider loving their city and community as part of their ministry – their Great Commission "to all nations" (Matt 28:19), those who have come from all over the world to live in their neighborhood. An attribute of a real Christ-follower and leader is one who knows the heart of God. Knowing God's heart is to reveal that God is love and only love (Nouwen, year, 25). He called us to love others, community, our neighbors, and our enemies because he loved us first. God's love is vast among our marginalized communities. "Grace is like water, it flows downhill and pools up in the lowest places" (Rocke & Van Dyk, 18).

Youth-Led Work Continues

SENTT adult allies have taken youth to city hall for planning commission meetings and city council meetings to have them gain first-hand experience on how to maneuver the system of local government. Adults need to create spaces and opportunities for our youth to be part of the decision-making process. So many decisions are made about them, without them. SENTT has been intentional about inviting other sister churches who have the same heart for community to join in the youth-led movement to create healthier neighborhoods. SENTT youth have co-facilitated trainings on advocacy during the spring break week for any church youth group interested in making positive changes in their own communities. Bethany Inner City Teen Night youth in downtown Fresno worked alongside the SENTT youth and in 2015 launched their own advocacy group called the Teen Night Transformation Team (TNTT). The SENTT and TNTT youth decided to combat the issue of negative advertising targeting youth and raised funds to rent five billboards all over southeast Fresno to showcase a positive message for six weeks during graduation season.

The Teen Night Transformation Team is now working on the issue of tobacco access and tobacco retailer saturation in Fresno. This work is being done as a collective impact model with the American Lung Association. Fresno Pacific University is also engaging in Christ-centered transformational work around their institution and will be with SENTT to address the issue of negative advertising around their neighborhood. Due to all of the SENTT leaders' tenacity, in December of 2015, after three years of youth work on the alcohol outlet saturation issue, there was a 7-0 vote on Alcohol access to youth in Fresno! The council members passed a resolution to move forward on a city ordinance that would change the current ABC CUP (conditional use permit) from a lifetime license to a five-year license that will be reviewed and take infractions into consideration before they are renewed. It will place restrictions on the proximity of alcohol retailers to schools, parks, youth spaces and other existing alcohol retailers so oversaturation doesn't occur. This is only the beginning and SENTT knows we have to continue the work with the elected officials to ensure that this ordinance comes to fruition. Onward!

Voices of Those Who Lead Us

As bi-vocational pastors who serve an impoverished and urban community, we have faced some difficulties full-time pastors do not generally encounter. We have limited financial resources and limited human resources requiring rigorous time management and balance between ministry and family life. Our greatest resource is a volunteer leadership team to help carry out the intentional and strategic planning to define the vision of UFCF. That is why the investment of time and effort we make in our young adult leaders for SENTT is vital to ensuring this faith and justice youth-led movement goes forward. I am compelled, and for a chapter like this it seems appropriate, to give them the last word ...

Anna Wells, SENTT Adult Ally, TNTT Founder, YLI Pink House Intern and Fresno City College student –

I am honored to walk alongside these amazing young people who are tapping into their potential and power to create healthy change in our community. I am constantly being challenged by their courage, perseverance, and faith as they stand up against some of the obstacles they face as young people in our community. During my time working with SENTT my faith has grown deeper and stronger as I learn what it means to do justice and seek the Shalom of our community from the incredible youth at SENTT!

Robert Vega, SENTT Adult Ally, Cambridge High School Teacher –
I love working with SENTT because it impacts our community in a positive way. I feel I have been very blessed in my life and I want to give back any way that I can. SENTT presents a great avenue to make a big difference. It is an investment in our youth and our neighborhoods. It has made me a better person, and I am thankful for that.

Jackie Buenuestro, SENTT Young Adult Ally, Fresno Pacific University Student –
In my short time as an adult ally with SENTT, I have not only fallen in love with the work but also with the youth and everyone involved. It has taught me the importance of voice and the immense impact it can have in a community if you take initiative. It has changed my perspective from waiting around thinking, "Someone should do this, if only someone could do this," to now WE should do this in order to better not only our our lives but those of everyone in this community. The youth in SENTT are truly inspiring, I see that no matter what struggles they have going on in their personal lives - at school, at home, at work, in relationships or struggles within - they always want to know what can they do now to help others around their community have a better and healthy life. The SENTT youth team has taught all the adults that get the honor to work with them the true definitions of selfless acts in God's name and with his grace. SENTT has actively been his hands and feet through every work they have done over the years and for generations

to come. Time after time, SENTT has clearly demonstrated what passion, dedication, and the love for God can accomplish.

Dallhana Garcia, SENTT Young Adult Ally, Fresno Pacific University Student -
Being a member of YLI youth council in high school allowed me to see the needs of community and the power of our voices; I learned that united we can make a difference. Now as an adult ally for SENTT, it is not solely about the ability to make a difference in our community, but the responsibility we have as Christians. When I began my faith journey, in college, I realized how imperative it was for us as the body of Christ to come together and care for our community along with our brothers and sisters in Christ. Isaiah 62:8 says, "For I, the Lord, love justice, I hate robbery and wrongdoing. In my faithfulness I will reward my people and make an everlasting covenant with them." Isaiah's was called to do justice work with faith, and I feel called to do the same. I cannot claim to love others if I am not caring for my community and my brothers and sisters that are invisible to the world, but precious in the eyes of the Lord. It is for this reason that I am strengthened to do work from Him, through Him and for Him, to ultimately bring Him all the honor, glory, and praise (Rom 11:36).

Monica Silva, SENTT Young Adult Ally, California State University, Fresno 2015 –
SENTT has transformed me and taught me to use my voice- written or spoken - to speak truth, love, and kindness into the lives of those around me. So often the underprivileged and broken-hearted are muted by the injustices in their lives. As such, they are bonded to poverty, unhappiness, violence, and disconnection. We must offer the same grace that has saved us, and lift up our brothers and sisters in Christ so they too may be heard and be counted.

John Mendez, SENTT Young Adult Ally, Fresno City College Student –

John 1:14 says the Word became flesh and made his dwelling among us. God, as Jesus, came down to dwell with his people. Jesus, dwelling with us, sought after us first in two ways. 1. He saw our physical needs and sicknesses and healed them. 2. He saw our spiritual needs and sicknesses and died on a cross as a perfect sacrifice justifying us being called children of God, thus healing us and restoring us to himself. The South East Neighborhood Transformation Team has taken Christ's model of holistic justice into their community. Ministry done this way is important to me because as a restored child of God, my involvement with SENTT has taken faith in Christ and our justification through him and applied that to those key principles by seeking the welfare of the community they serve.

Works Cited

Alaniz, M.L. and Wilkes, C. (1995). Reinterpreting Latino Culture in the Commodity Form: The Case of Alcohol Advertising in the Mexican American Community. *Hispanic Journal of Behavioral Sciences,* 17 (4):430–451.

Bakke, Raymond J. (1997). *A Theology as Big as the City.* Downers Grove, IL: InterVarsity Press.

Clark, Chap and Powell, Kara (2007). *Deep Justice in a Broken World.* Grand Rapids, IL: Zondervan.

Committee on Public Education (1999). Media Education. *American Association of Pediatrics, 104 (2),* 341-343.

Eccles, J. & Gootman, J.A. (Eds.). (2002). *Community Programs to Promote Youth Development.* Washington, D.C.: National Academy Press.

Factfinder.census.gov, Nov. 2015.

Gambone, M.A., Klem, A.M. & Connell, J.P. (2002). *Finding Out What Matters for Youth: Testing Key Links in a Community Action Framework for Youth.* Philadelphia, PI: Youth Development Strategies, Inc.

Gruenewald, P.J. and Remer, L. (2004). Changes in outlet densities affect violence rates. *Alcoholism: Clinical and Experimental Research, 30 (7),* 1184-1193.

McLaughlin, M. (2000). Community Counts: How Youth Organizations Matter for Youth Development. *Educational Resources Information Center.* Washington D.C.: Public Education Network.

Nouwen, Henri. (1999). *In the Name of Jesus – Reflections on Christian Leadership.* Chestnut Ridge, NY: Crossroads Publishing.

Pittman, K. and Martin, S. (2007, July) *Core Principles for Engaging Young People in Community Change*. Washington, D.C.: The Forum for Youth Investment, Impact Strategies, Inc.

Rocke, Kris; Van Dyke, Joel. (2012). *Geography of Grace*. Tacoma, WA: Street Psalms Press.

Nieves, Evelyn. (2005, November 21). In Fresno, Tackling Poverty Moves to the Top of the Agenda. *The Washington Post*. http://www.washingtonpost.com/ wp-dyn/content/article/2005/11/20/ AR2005112001018.html

Chapter Six

Using Data in Service of Community Transformation

Jacob Huang

Assistant Professor of Sociology, Fresno Pacific University

> *"It is a capital mistake to theorize before one has data."*
>
> Sir Arthur Conan Doyle

Data is Not the Plural of Anecdote

In the world of faith, sometimes motivation is regarded as more important than outcomes, intent is rated higher than results, and a few anecdotal stories of success unfortunately supplant empirical data as a basis for future strategy. Churches and faith-based community benefit organizations (F-CBOs) are willing to initiate a community movement and to deepen their influences in a community because their service based on biblical values mobilizes visible resources (such as a place and donated goods) and invisible resources (such as volunteers and networking). For many Christians, serving in the community is not only a way of benefitting others, but also a way of practicing faith in God. The command to *"Love your neighbor as yourself"* (Mark 12:31) and the parable of the Good Samaritan tend to be common ground for F-CBOs proposing various community ministries. With these as motivation, it can become easy for F-CBOs to rest on the inherent justification of good motivations, whether or not their service was relevant or actually making the measureable difference they intend. Worse yet, without measurement, we assume and we believe but we cannot confirm whether the approaches are effective or not. As Jim Fruchterman has shown,

Many nonprofit program teams simply assume that their work has lasting impact, typically without conducting additional studies to find out if that is actually the case. Many nonprofits are founded to meet an acute need in society: They see a hole that needs filling and fill it. They heal the sick, feed the hungry, house the homeless, and educate the uneducated. They experience the rewards of seeing transformation on the ground. They know they are making a difference. Unfortunately, that might not be the case. Many randomized control trials have been conducted on social programs that found no effect. That is, something that the program staff was sure was making a difference, wasn't. (2016, 1).

But the fact is, as he goes on to say, "Data will make the work of social change agents more effective and will build the case for support for the best programs and enterprises" (Fruchterman, 2016, 1).

Commonly, many churches believe they should step out of the door of the church and reach out to those in need in the community. Since the ministry of community service is spiritually motivated, F-CBOs leaders are more dedicated to creating strategies in a project that can reflect their values and beliefs. While celebrating the emerging projects that bring much excitement and joy to the community, we rarely look back at those dying projects and many F-CBOs that are facing a number of challenges every day, including the complexity of raising funds, a shortage of staff, volunteers, facilities, irrelevance, and places where they have missed the mark. Moreover, even though F-CBOs can see needs in the community, they are often limited in their ability to identify common characteristics among those in need and where these community members are located (see Appendix I).

The Neighborhood Church in Fresno, California, believes church ministry in a contemporary society should not be limited to a single building; instead, church ministries should be more contextualized and rooted in community. In fact, this church is organized around a specific community—the Jackson Neighborhood, perhaps the most ethnically and class diverse neighborhood in the city. Their belief is that church ministries should let the neighborhood speak about their needs and desires. Each Christian's residence in the neighborhood is like a candle of God's love and care, listening to neighbors' material and spiritual needs and making disciples. That means a basic unit in community, a Christian household, can be a mediator that is reaching out to neighbors, initiating neighborhood ministries, and practice God's love. Church, as a holy family of Christians, disbursed and scattered throughout the neighborhood, is also an important resource for community residents. In order to support sufficient resources for Christian families to initiate and sustain their ministries, The Neighborhood Church found that a community survey was helpful so community information and resources can be shared with each other. By using free-access applications, such as the U.S. Census, Google Map, and Healthycity.org, the church was able to complete a demographic report on the Jackson Neighborhood and the report has become an important basis for applicable neighborhood ministries. They learned how many homes were in the eight by twelve block section that comprised the neighborhood. They sketched those residents' racial/ethnic characteristics. They saw the level of educational attainment, which led to becoming involved with the school, and also started working on creating a vocational mentoring program. They probed income statistics, which gave them insight into the class divisions by street. They were sympathetic with employment challenges faced by the residents, which led them to plan for the start of a social business. Data is serving the mission of this church plant.

On the other hand, without an approach like that, when engaging in community projects F-CBOs may overestimate their ability to fully execute projects or may plan approaches that are inappropriate or unsustainable. Unless F-CBOs are very sensitive with what the purposes of the community ministries are, what assets and resources they hold in hand, and who they are going to serve, serious miscalculations are likely. For instance, in a well-known Vietnamese immigrant community in Seattle, Washington, a church intended to establish an ESL (English as Second Language) program for immigrants who have limited English proficiency. As many congregations might, the church assumed the language ministry can be a useful approach to meet the residents' needs. After they recruited qualified teachers, prepared sufficient materials, set up class-settings and advertised the program extensively in the Vietnamese community, no one showed up. The church's leaders admirably did follow-up in the community, and were told that even though the language ministry was quite meaningful for the Vietnamese residents, their primary felt-need was having affordable childcare, which would allow them greater flexibility to work. The felt-need was financial. Church leaders can sometimes be limited by their assumptions and previous church experiences instead of being sensitive to unique characteristics and needs of community residents based on objective information. Without objective data, significant questions are left unasked: Do we really serve the right people? Are there services already provided by other community organizations? What strengths exist here that could be built upon? Since answers to these questions are left unasked, church and faith-based organization leaders can be limited in their perspective. As recently noted, "Most social sector staff and managers struggle with data: getting it, ... using it correctly" (Fruchterman, 2016, 1).

Moreover, F-CBOs are often passive in their approach to information from other institutions or sources. Each piece of information is like a piece of a puzzle providing a correct image of the community, but decisions are often made without the benefit of the whole picture. In the absence of analyzing community data, F-CBOs can be limited in their ability to know where resources are shared and exchanged, where people are in need, what community strengths are, and what changes are aspired to by the community.

Using Data Analysis

While people in ministry may not be inclined toward data analysis, practitioners recognize the insights provided by increasingly accessible data tools as incredibly valuable. By using basic data analysis, leaders and other practitioners of community services can get a better sense of available resources and needs in a community and can create a portrait of reality based in fact.

However, there are three common hurdles facing many F-CBOs regarding data. First, in terms of human resources and equipment, does using data analysis necessarily require hiring information technicians (ITs) or having advanced computer skills? Second, will data access be expensive? Third, is it possible to create new community data for the needs of the organization rather than relying on secondary data?

Fortunately, technology for data analysis is easier to access than it was a couple decades ago. Much data about local communities has been freely released for public use. Accessing this data does not necessarily require advanced computer skills and equipment. Many sources of data provided by authorities such as federal/state governments and national organizations are very reliable and updated on time. F-CBOs can even build their own database for their specific needs by using open-access platforms. For this reason, use of data can be a helpful tool that improves the effectiveness of community ministry.

Knowing Your Community

In this section I will introduce resources designed to collect community data, and discuss components of data analysis for community transformation in the U.S. The first rule of thumb is that data must serve the mission; its acquisition is not a valuable end in itself. For practitioners, the data and the technology tools used to collect it are only valuable inasmuch as they lead to more effectively serving people.

Literally, data analysis is composed of two concepts, "data" and "analysis." In the context of this chapter, data refers to any information about a community, its demography, or social realities and characteristics. Community data is often collected by either authorities or community organizations, but can also simply be the result of the organized efforts of neighbors. The quality of data collected determines the validity of any analysis that emerges. Analysis is a way of explaining collected community data, and again this can happen in the context of a dedicated group of leaders in a neighborhood focused church or other F-CBOs. Through the analysis, various characteristics of a community can be demonstrated, which can lead to more effective decision-making. Therefore, where to find reliable community data, how to build self-constructed data, and how to present community data are three essential ways data can assist in knowing a community.

Three Types and Sources of Community Data

General Survey Data: The first type of community data is based on a general survey of a population, such the U.S. Census. This type of data demonstrates a general overview of demography in a community, such as gender, age, education, and race/ethnicity. This type of data is usually descriptive, such as the number of men and women living in a community, education of community residents across different levels in percentage, housing status in percentage among residents, and general health status of residents. Accessing this type of community data from open access platforms can help F-CBO practitioners grasp quick facts with a macro view of the community.

The U.S. Census. Since 1790, the U.S. Census Bureau has conducted a general survey of the population once every decade. The Bureau releases data, available on its website, for the general public in the following categories: population, emergency preparedness, housing, employment, income & poverty, families/living arrangements, education, and health. Based on the needs of community organizations, the data can describe general information of neighborhoods in city/county, state, or the nation (see Figure 1).

In addition, the website provides an application which allows users to construct quick facts online based on the results of the U.S. Census and to download the selected facts from the website. At the same time, the selected data can be presented in various formats, including maps (in cooperation with Google Maps), charts, and statistical tables. Data is easily accessible. Many people with middle school math skills can read and understand a community's information by using data from the U.S. Census. Practitioners can quickly learn about the social characteristics of community residents to develop more appropriate strategies for community services. In addition, the U.S. Census Bureau also provides raw data (original data before being processed) with a spreadsheet format for the general public to download. Downloading from the website, F-CBOs can process the public data in order to better understand the community environment.

On the other hand, since the public data is descriptive for each individual category, such as age, gender, and race/ethnicity, when F-CBOs seek to know more stratified information, such as percentage of women with college education in a community or average size of families in poverty, the application on the website may not offer sufficient technical support to process the complex data. In other words, advanced statistical skills and applications (such as Microsoft Excel, SPSS, SAS, R, and STATA) may be needed to process the community data. Thankfully, churches are often rich repositories of the skill sets one might need to use those data tools, and some parishioners use them as part of their professions. Moreover, the U.S. Census Bureau defines boundaries among small areas by creating census tracts. Census tracts are polygons based upon geographic environments, usually smaller than 8,000 residents, and are therefore more likely to generate accurate demographic data. Unlike zip codes as clusters of lines (defined by the U.S. Post Service), sometimes areas based on census tracts might not mesh exactly with zip codes. While using the U.S. Census online applications, community data might not be able to present variations between clusters of zip codes rather than cities and counties. If F-CBOs want to know further information about a zip-code-based neighborhood, it is necessary to download the raw data from the website and then use advanced applications for data analysis.

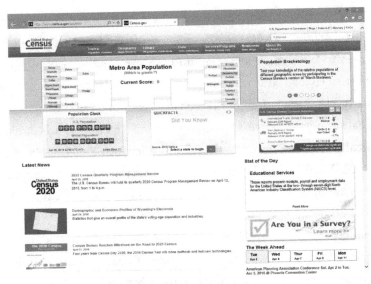

(Figure 1. Homepage of the U.S. Census)

American Community Survey. In order to better understand current conditions in, and the perspective of a community, the U.S. Census Bureau also conducts the American Community Survey (ACS, see Figure 2). Unlike the U.S. Census, which is conducted once every ten years, ACS is an annual survey. Also, using methods of sampling, ACS employs data from selected samples for the same cubic areas (census tracts and block groups) consistently. The collected data is used to predict the development of a community in one, three, and five years, respectively. In other words, although not everyone is surveyed in the ACS, due to restrictions of research design and methodology, the survey still provides reliable current community data and development estimates of the community in terms of demographic, economic, housing as well as social characteristics, such as education, marital status, and citizenship status.

There are two ways to access ACS data. First, on the website of ACS, users can create a table for profiles of a specific community (county/city). At the same time, if needed, other characteristics or areas can be added into the same table for comparative analysis. This is relatively easy, and is useful to build a data-driven profile. Second, like the U.S. Census, users can freely download raw data with spreadsheets from the ACS website. Again, advanced statistical skills and applications may be needed for processing selected data. Like the U.S. Census, when users access the online application for data analysis, the basic unit of community is city/county rather than a zip-code-based neighborhood. If needed, users can download the data from the website and then use computer applications to further analyze the community data.

(Figure 2. Homepage of the American Community Survey)

American Housing Survey. Another survey conducted by the U.S. Census Bureau is the American Housing Survey (AHS, see Figure 3). AHS is a biennial national survey that collects comprehensive information on housing, such as number of units in a household, ownership, location, years built, and neighborhood shopping in selected regions or metropolitan areas. The website releases up-to-date housing data with spreadsheets and reports for the general public. Finding out the housing realities of a particular community leads to a myriad of other forms of data, including percentage of income used for housing, which gives insight into one aspect of the pressures faced by residents. Users can work on basic data analysis through Microsoft Excel in a local computer's hard drive. Unfortunately, this survey does not provide an online application for data analysis.

In addition, health data is often used to project the quality of a population in a community. For community transformation, the physical health of residents is an important indicator to evaluate the sustainability of a community. For F-CBOs, health data can be used to illustrate potential material needs and health risks for community residents in terms of access to healthy food, medical resources, and health risks in the community. The Centers for Disease Control and Prevention (CDC) releases related health data presented in various formats, such as complete reports, charts, maps, and tables, on their website. Once F-CBOs design any health-related community ministries/services, the website can be a useful hub for searching necessary health data.

Public Attitudes On Social Topics

The second type of community data explores attitudes of the general public on social topics. Usually, this type of data provides further cross-stratified information about what kind of people are more likely to support/oppose certain social issues. In other words, an F-CBO's services sometimes might focus too much on its own missions/objectives rather than attitudes of community residents. That can make ministry-focused community services ineffective by not receiving input from community residents.

In order to reduce the gap between F-CBOs and community residents, analysis for this type of data can inspire the leadership to develop more applicable strategies in a neighborhood. In other words, besides F-CBOs' mission and objectives, the voice of residents in a community, should be heard by community service providers and practitioners.

(Figure 3. Homepage of American Housing Survey)

General Social Survey. Since 1972, the General Social Survey (GSS, see Figure 4) has been conducted to monitor comprehensive societal changes in demographic, behavioral, and attitudinal questions as well as some special topics in the United States. The survey is conducted by the National Data Program for the Social Sciences led by the National Opinion Research Center (NORC), a social science research center at the University of Chicago with the support of the National Science

Foundation. Before 1991, the survey was conducted annually and after 1991 the survey has been conducted once every other year. In fact, the main feature of the survey is its special topics, including religiosity, religious identity, climate change, quality of life, and psychological well-being, and so on.

Moreover, in order to share the benefits of the data analysis with the general public, a new website, GSS Data Explorer, provides a user-friendly interface for searching variables that can help users grasp up-to-date opinions of the general public and also presents or visualizes the collected data analysis. In other words, besides downloading existing reports of GSS data analysis free of charge, users can also create a free account and create their own project online.

Another advantage of the survey is its cross-national data. As part of the International Survey Program, GSS in the United States and social surveys in fifty-eight other nations are sharing similar survey structures so that data can be analyzed and compared between nations. However, unlike the other surveys, this survey is not able to present the data specifically at a city/county level. Instead, stratification of geography in the U.S. is divided into ten regions (such as New England, Middle Atlantic, East North, South Atlantic, Central, West North Central, East South Central, West South Central, Mountain, and Pacific). Although the survey might not directly provide city/county data, city/county-based community organizations can still oversee changes and trends of a region or a whole society.

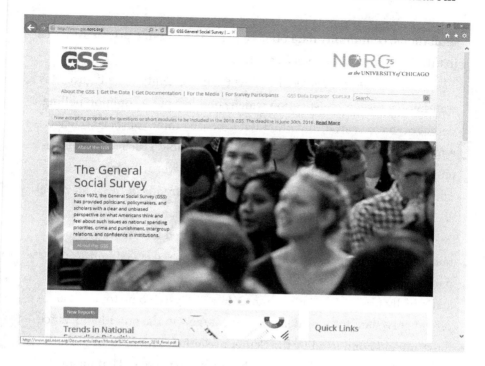

(Figure 4. Homepage of General Social Survey)

Data Generated and Managed by Private Institutions

The third type of community data is that generated by privately-owned institutions, such as a corporation or a think tank. This type of data might not necessarily be released to the general public. Instead, some data is only exchanged and shared between providers and users based on confidential agreements. In order to access community data with confidential information, users sometimes need to pay fees and make a legal agreement with data providers. Moreover, although some data generated by private institutions is released publically without fees-based services, the general public might still be restricted in accessing updated community data. Although there are potential uncertainties and restrictions for users of community organizations with financial

197

limitations, community data offered by some reputable private research institutions can still be seen as a reliable resource.

Pew Research Center. The Pew Research Center (see Figure 5) is a well-known research institution which conducts public opinion polling, demographic research, and other data-focused topics of social science. As a nonprofit fact tank funded by the Pew Charitable Trusts, their results of data analysis have become an important non-governmental source to understand attitudes of the general public and trends of U.S. and global society for policy making as well as for public dialogs.

As a fact tank, the center provides analyzed information. That means that for the general public, widely-discussed social topics such as parenting, religion, use of technology, and political polling are statistically presented. For advanced data analysis, some topics also provide raw data for download free of charge. On the other hand, since most surveys conducted by the Center are either nationally or globally focused, the results are based on a broader perspective. That means that for county/city-based community organizations, the results are more beneficial for understanding changes and trends in the overall U.S. society rather than of residents in any single cities, counties, or states.

In addition, some non-governmental organizations establish platforms in which the general public can access and present community data from multiple governmental resources. Many websites are user-friendly in that people are not required to have any statistical background. Even though the governmental data is accurate, users still need to be aware when the data managed by the non-governmental organizations was last updated.

(Figure 5. Homepage of the Pew Research Center)

US Boundary.com. This website (see Figure 6) provides a tool in which users can build a graph of the community with integrated community information, such as schools, health care services, voting districts, and post service areas. For community service practitioners, the website is a beneficial tool for accessing community data from various

sources. Also, users can freely download or share the outputs with other social media for their use. Regarding characteristics of community data, this website mainly offers descriptive community information. That means the website does not provide community data which has been analyzed across social stratifications, such as the average percentage of women in a community. Therefore, this website is for accessing basic demographic community information.

(Figure 6. Homepage of USBoundary.com)

Building Your Own Community Data

As noted, use of technology is an effective way to access community data from governmental authorities and non-governmental organizations. However, due to the unique characteristics of F-CBOs, community data offered by a single source might not fully meet the needs of the community organization. There are more resources that F-CBOs can use to build and manage their own community data. Therefore, in order to encourage community organizations to conduct their own research of the community, some websites provide useful tools that F-CBOs can use to construct their own community data for their particular strategies in community services.

Healthycity.org. Moreover, some websites provide state-wide data that can be localized to a particular community. The website of Healthcity.org (see Figure 7) provides a platform in which public users can gather and sort factors influencing a community's health, including facts about housing, education, foster care, economics, safety, population characteristics, and services in a community. Looking at a community through these lenses opens up our perspective significantly. Data on this website is visual. By integrating demographic data and spatial data, the relative health of a community can be presented using maps. The maps are highly customizable, enabling the user to draw their own boundary lines, making the data more specific to the community being studied. The importance of this cannot be overstated. Registered users can even build and upload self-investigated data to the website. Although the website basically only offers information in California, Healthcity.org arranges a platform that website designers, data authorities, and public users in community services can use to share, exchange, and update community data with each other. Other states will eventually develop these. In other words, community data can be more interactive and allow F-CBOs to be more proactive in building and sharing their community data. A similar website, Healthlandscape.org, provides health-related data only in West Virginia (see Figure 8).

(Figure 7. Homepage of HealthyCity.org)

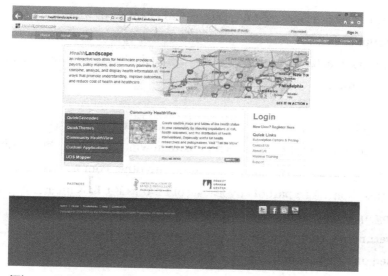

(Figure 8. Homepage of Healthlandscape.org)

The non-governmental organizations' websites of community data are designed to be more user-friendly. Many people with basic computing skills can access, read, and interpret most results of community data. The risk users might have to face is whether the data is updated in a timely manner. Unlike governmental resources, data from these websites might not be updated as frequently because they don't have consistent funding support. Therefore, while using the services, F-CBOs should always check if the data is from a reliable source and how frequently it's updated.

Fresno Community Scorecard is a typical example of nonprofit organizations and higher educational institutions collaborating to establish a system to present facts and resources in Fresno, California (see Figure 9). People, agriculture, culture and quality of life, economic vitality, education, equity, health, housing, safe community, strong families, and sustainable infrastructure are included. Based on a user-friendly interface, community residents can easily look up current statistic data of the community and a list of available institutional

203

resources. This scorecard format is a good example of what your community can accomplish via a collaborative approach between educational institutions, the Business Council, a regional foundation, and other entities.

(Figure 9. Homepage of Fresno Community Scorecard)

Community Commons is a website in which users can build, save, and share community data investigated with other community organizations. As a part of advocacy, sometimes F-CBOs might need to bring up some community issues that need attention from residents, governments, and other interested organizations. Because the service is based on collaboration among organizations in a community, networking

with other local organizations can be an important component for building a community project (see Figure 10).

(Figure 10. Homepage of Community Commons)

Dr. Bruce Jackson of Collaborative Community Transformation has listed less formal forms of data collection, such as community surveys and on-the-street interviews, that could be helpful for the technologically challenged. These interviews are conversational, without clipboard in hand, and the questions cover topics that will require a debrief later. A church team could handle them, and then collate the perspectives gathered to help inform a community transformation approach, eventually even in a collaborative posture with the very people they interviewed. They include questions such as, "What gets you excited about the neighborhood? What is depressing about the neighborhood? What are its strengths? What are its most pressing needs? How has the neighborhood changed since you've been here? What people or

205

organizations have been the biggest blessing here?" and many others.
These and other potential questions are included in Appendix II.

Infogr.am is a website which offers tools for public organizations to
create charts and infographics of their data (see Figure 11). The website is
able to optimize community data selected by the community
organizations for visualization in charts and graphics. The data output
can also be directed to social media, such as Twitter, Facebook, Linkedin,
and Google +, so that users under the same system can share and
exchange data and presentations with each other.

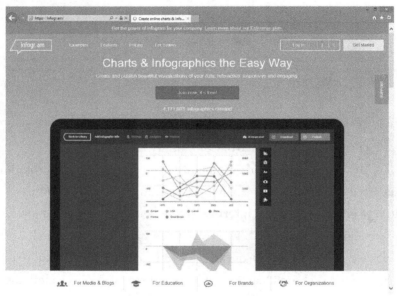

(Figure 11. Homepage of Infogr.am)

With a global influence, *Google's My Maps* provides applications
with a lower cost or even free services for public users to generate their
own community data (see Figure 12). Google Maps integrates its existing
resources to provide a base map and registered users can create layers by
implementing photos, texts, and so on to represent their own
communities. Like other Google products, users in My Maps can

collaborate with each other on the same project. The main disadvantage of My Maps is that users need to employ first-hand data, such as photos and texts, to generate a layer, instead of accessing data from other sources. Otherwise, My Maps has a user-friendly interface in which community organizations can build community data either on their own

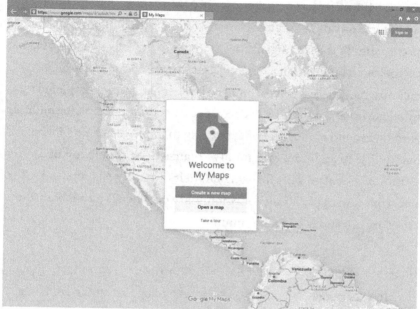

or in collaboration with other organizations.

(Figure 12. My Maps)

To ensure the quality of data analysis generated by other sources, community organizations need to be aware of whether community data is provided by reputable authorities. A simple way to evaluate the reputation of data providers is to investigate if the data provider is funded by a public interest organization, such as governments and educational/academic institutions, or by personal/commercial interest organization, such as companies and personal blogs. Although data provided by the authorities is reliable, the data sometimes might not fully present information of a local community where community organizations are situated. When community organizations cannot find a suitable person with basic statistical training to process the data, they might lose their capacity to access data from the reliable institutions.

On the other hand, if community organizations plan to build their own community data for analysis, networking with other organizations in the community is a significant way to improve the effectiveness of using free tools and applications. Organizations in the community must recognize that successful community services cannot be completed by any single organization. Instead, consistent communication for building common ground is the most effective way to improve benefits for the community. In addition, community organizations should not be institutional-centric, only focusing on their own interests. Instead, use of these tools and applications for community data needs a collaboration across organizations in the community.

Conclusion: Beyond Community Data Analysis

In the past decade, F-CBOs have taken huge advantage of using technology, such as new social media that can improve and promote their ministry services in the community. The users, especially younger generations, are more likely to access ministry information and to join the ministry from F-CBOs' websites, Facebook, Twitter, and so on. However, for community organizations, use of new technology should not be used only to appeal potential members. Technology can also be used to assist community organizations in generating and analyzing community data now, not only for deeply and meaningfully understanding their communities but also for seeking opportunities of cooperation among community organizations.

In other words, use of community data analysis can help community organizations know what a community is like, what its people face on a daily basis, and where resources can be found. In order to optimize community data applied to strategies of community ministry, it is suggested that F-CBOs should consider how to build, access, and manage reliable community data. As a logistical support, community data either generated by themselves or in collaboration with other community organizations, colleges, universities, or governments can provide F-CBOs more accurate information to place resources effectively. Community data management is a platform for F-CBOs to build, process, and update community information, such as demography, living environment, public opinion, and available resources with each other.

As mentioned, many sources of community data are accurate and easy for community organizations to access. Free tools and applications are available for community organizations to process with low cost. These resources are freely provided, but are not cheaply made. F-CBOs should step forward to use data analysis for improving strategies for community transformation.

"Let the community, itself, speak!" said Joe White, Pastor of the Neighborhood Church. He noted that when F-CBOs use community data analysis, they are enabled to more clearly hear the voice of the community, and strategies can be fashioned to work with the community to see it flourish. As a result, ministries guided by a vision of a community transformed can anchor their dreams and give them birth in the realities – the assets and needs and leadership – of the neighborhood itself.

Works Cited

Fruchterman, Jim, (Summer 2016). Using Data for Action and for
    Impact, *Stanford Social Innovation Review*, Retrieved from
    https://ssir.org/articles/entry/using_data_for_action_and_for
    _impact

See also appendix for relevant websites

Appendix I. Sources of Community Data and Tools/Applications				
Website	Data/ Service Provider Affiliation	Category	Raw Data Available ?	Link
The US Census	US Census Bureau	Demography	V	http://www.census.gov/en.html
American Community Survey	US Census Bureau	Demography	V	https://www.census.gov/programs-surveys/acs/
American Housing Survey	US Census Bureau	Housing	V	http://www.census.gov/programs-surveys/ahs.html
CDC Health Data and Statistics	The Centers for Disease Control and Prevention	Health	V	http://www.cdc.gov/DataStatistics/
General Social Survey	NORC, Social Science Research Center, at the University of Chicago, and National Science Foundation	Social trend and social issues	V	https://gssdataexplorer.norc.org/
Pew Research Center	Pew Charitable Trusts	Social trend and social issues	V	http://www.pewforum.org/
US Boundary.com		Integrated demographic data		http://www.usboundary.com/
Healthycity.org		Integrated health data in California		http://healthycity.org
Fresno Community Scorecard		Integrated demographic data in Fresno, CA		http://www.fresnoscorecard.org/

Healthlandscape.org		Integrated health data in West Virginia		http://healthlandscape.org
Community Commons		To build a community report		http://www.communitycommons.org/
Infogr.am		To build community charts		https:// infogr.am
My Maps	Google	To build community maps		https://www.google.com/maps/d/?hl=en_US&app =mp

Appendix II: On the street interviews: The following questions are suggestions; be creative in asking questions that pertain directly to the person and the flow of the conversation. Source: Dr. Bruce Jackson – Collaborative Community Transformation Dissertation (download here: http://www.mediafire.com/file/v46fyut1sbccw1n/Jac)

Open the conversation by asking if you could talk with the person about the community; you simply want to learn about his or her experience from living/working in the community. The flow of the conversations should typically be questions from general to specific. Try not to ask narrowly focused questions; instead ask questions that are open-ended. Ask follow-up questions to gain a clearer understanding and perspective.

Initially ask questions to understand the individual and his involvement in the neighborhood/community.

How long have you lived/worked here?

What attracted (drew, caused) you to move here?

What was the neighborhood like when you first moved in?

How has it changed?

What gets you excited about the neighborhood?

What is depressing about the neighborhood?

Next begin to gain her perspective of the community:

What are the strengths/What do you like?

How would you describe the community?

What do you not like/what are the weaknesses?

Ask community-specific questions:

What do you see as the greatest needs of the community?

What are the greatest concerns?

How would you describe the community?

What are the top concerns of the neighborhood?

How are the churches involved in the community?

What ways have you benefited from the church being in the community?

What business, associations, organizations have been a benefit to the community? Are there those that have been a detriment to the community?

What would be important for me to know in order to better understand/get to know the community?

Chapter Seven

Embedding a Legacy of Hope in Your City Through Asset Based Community Development

Monika Grasley

LifeLine CDC, Merced, CA

> *"The hard truth is that development must start from within the community and, in most of our urban neighborhoods, there is no other choice."*
>
> Jody Kretzmann & John McKnight

Created in the Image of God

As I walk through the entrance of our regional mens' prison I wonder what I have to share with people who are incarcerated. I hear the clanging of the electronic, barred doors as they open and shut behind me and I see the barbed wire that is keeping the inmates far away from my community. And yet, here I am.

This group of "lifers" I am to address comes together as part of their rehabilitation. They are waiting for years, often decades, to be allowed a board hearing and yet there is something about these men that seems freer than many people I have met on the outside. While they are behind fences and walls, many seem to have made peace with their situation, while I see people daily on the outside who have all the freedom they want, but are living in anger, frustration and unrest.

So I begin sharing my life story, a story of abuse, shame, guilt and loss of innocence. I share with them about the labels people have put on me and I have put on myself, like poor, victim, homeless, and uneducated. Sticky labels now cover me and I wonder what labels have been put on the fifty men I see before me.

At LifeLine we are reminded that everyone has a story; that nobody wakes up one day and commits a crime, becomes a drug addict, lives in poverty. We are reminded that the story can always be changed.

I start exchanging my labels: my "abuse" label becomes "empathetic;" my "lack of education" becomes "innovative." And so I exchange every label for something positive, not because I am pretending to be someone else, but because I see myself differently now. I am rewriting my story in light of the Story written by the author of life. I ask the prisoners to write down some of the gifts they have and they begin to rewrite their own stories.

I share with them that Genesis chapter one says we are created in the image of God and that we all have God's DNA inside of us. Our story is larger than our failures. We talk about being created by God in our mother's womb (Ps 139), that God was there from the beginning, that we are not accidents but that God designed the time, date of birth, and parents we were going to have. We talk about being God's workmanship (masterpiece), created in Christ Jesus to do good works that God prepared in advance for us to do (Eph 2:10).

As I continue to talk I see a change happening in the group. Some of the men are sitting up a little straighter; a couple of them wipe their eyes as they realize they are not just the crime they committed.

The way we see ourselves really determines the outcome of our lives. For too long we have labeled people: criminal, single mom, homeless, drug addict, bad neighborhood, non- Christian, or poor. Most people, myself included, tend to live into those labels. The same is true for communities. Winton, one of the communities we work with, is known for its gangs, drugs, and crime. It even made national news a few years back as a "Meth Capital."

But we find ourselves compelled by the question, "What if we change the narrative?" What if we could see people with their stories and help them rediscover their giftedness through the struggle of life? What if we intentionally looked for the assets present in their lives, instead of just a litany of needs?

I am ready to leave the prison and some of the men come up to me and thank me for the reminder that they are still human beings, that they still have gifts and skills and abilities and that their labels do not have to define them. They share about the legacies they want to leave for their own families, the next generation of men incarcerated, the world around them. Now I am the one with tears in my eyes, as one by one they come, shake my hand, and thank me for the reminder.

All of us need to rediscover the dignity we have, taking the old labels and replacing them with something new. We don't ignore what has happened but we recognize God is still in the process of redemption and restoration of individual lives and whole communities.

As I walk out of the prison through the barbed wire and the security gates I wonder if that part of the prison looks a little bit more like God's kingdom. When Jesus taught us to pray he said, "Your kingdom come, Your will be done on earth as it is in heaven." Maybe those fifty men got to see a little more of heaven this evening.

A city transforms when we see the gifts, assets, and skills of everyone and when people, no matter their walk of life, are treated with dignity. But when we see people as projects, when we think we can fix them, when we think that we have all the solutions - then we are creating consumers. People who wait for a hand-out are paralyzed and can't move forward without our attention. But if we see people as capable human beings who are active participants in their own well-being and the well-being of their community, then we are joining together as citizens to leave a greater legacy of health and beauty around us. *We leave a legacy in the city when each person recognizes he is created in the image of God and he has something to contribute to his neighborhood.* How does it happen? Here a few lessons I learned over the last few years.

Learn to be become a better listener

As we began to explore the small town of Winton we came with good intentions, dreams of making a real difference, and plenty of ideas, but we also knew we were coming in as learners and listeners, as "newbies" to the neighborhood. I did not understand the cultural implications of poverty, the different worldview and social norms that governed many people in this town. I did not understand the various ethnic groups that were present and I did not understand the many community dynamics. While I thought I came in with a humble heart and a learning spirit, in hindsight, it was really more of a superiority model and a savior complex. I have learned much over the years, but not a day goes by that I don't discover something else I don't know or make another mistake. And that is OK. God has given me little glimpses of hope throughout this initial journey: A community member who promises to pray, a deep conversation about spiritual warfare, and dear friends from all over who actively pray and support the work God has called me to here. *To leave a legacy in a city we need to obey God's call. We need to be willing to watch and learn and enter into a humbling exercise that reminds us we do not know it all.*

Walk and Pray - Get God's Point of View

When we entered the community we wanted to get God's heartbeat for the neighborhood, so we walked and prayed. We listened to God's voice and asked for eyes to see what He sees. We prayed for the people, looking for open doors to engage with folks as we experienced Winton.

Winton was known as a high-crime, high-drug, high-unemployment town but we wanted to see the other side of it. We had done the demographic analysis and learned about the history and crime statistics. But we saw more: small ethnic restaurants with enticing aromas, people sitting outside having conversations, kids walking to school, moms hanging out their laundry. We wanted to see what God sees.

When we want to see Christ-centered city transformation we first need to see through Jesus's eyes. We need to see the love Jesus has for the city and for the people. As we were getting to know the people of Winton, they got to know us, conveying in many ways that they were watching us, and waiting to see what would happen. This was the predominant attitude at first. They had seen too many groups come in wanting to change things, bringing in programs, evaluating their needs to fix them only to abandon them soon after the money ran out or the grant was completed. So the people watched and waited. *Leaving a legacy means we stick around, we don't give up when things get tough, we don't walk away when we are not the heroes of the story. Leaving a legacy means we stay as long as God says "stay."*

A Place to Belong

When we first started working in Winton we had access to a space that had already become a gathering place. This little 1,000-

square-foot space has become a place of action. In the first year we started building trusting relationships with community members. When the time came to dream a little bigger I led a group of community members through a visioning exercise. Men, women, young and old, ex-drug addicts and felons, business people and unemployed came together to dream about what they wanted Winton to look like. In the end it came down to this: "We want to put Winton on the map for something good."

Embedding hope in a community means we help people see what they already have, and that begins when we bring them together. They begin to see each other as the change agents of their communities. We do this by creating a space for conversation, where people can get together, dream, and learn from each other. They start working together for the good of their own community. We come alongside with some of our gifts and skills (for example, basic group facilitation methods, planning guides, connections) and we all work together for a better community. *Empowering community members with tools and access to resources is the best way to ensure the sustainability of community transformation.*

Making some hard decisions

After six months in the community of Winton I led a process closing down the only food pantry in town, successfully alienating many community members. How's that for a beginning? Drive down any street in Winton and you will see cars under perpetual repair, fences covered in graffiti, some quite elaborate, others little more than branding. You'll see youth wandering aimlessly. Winton is a small, unincorporated town of 8,000 people. Initially it was a thriving small community with a train station that transported the rich agricultural produce the Central Valley grew. A vibrant Air Force community then enhanced the agricultural setting. But when the Air Force base closed 20 years ago, it left this small town with little to build upon. Migrant workers made this their seasonal home and some stayed and built homes for themselves. Established community members tried to invest into their community but Winton was also becoming a turf battle for rival gangs and a thoroughfare for drug trafficking. Over the years the more established families felt overtaken by gangs, drugs and violence. Since Winton is unincorporated much of the infrastructure needed to create a healthy vibrant community was lacking. No sidewalks or lights, no real job opportunities, and many families living in the shadows because of their immigration status created a perfect storm for gangs to overtake Winton and for many people to stop caring. It seemed like we had just been handing out band-aids.

A ministry started by a pastor many years ago had great programs to keep children and youth in a safe environment and helped them with life skills, but over the years the pastor had to step back, leaving this small center more a food pantry than anything else. We were asked if we would be interested in investing into the community of Winton.

The pantry was everyone's favorite program. Volunteers drove to Modesto and Turlock every week to gather donated foods. Others set up assembly stations for the food boxes. Dozens of families used the pantry, many every week. But the food that was given out was often expired or it was unhealthy junk food. If we believe in the dignity of people then they should not have to get our leftovers. It was a hard decision to shut it down, but we had to begin to address the problems in the community in a more holistic way.

Find the Assets Around You

Winton is a small unincorporated town in the central valley, made up of wonderful community members from different walks of life:

undocumented residents, established farmers, small business owners, senior citizens, and young people. But there has not been a lot of infrastructure, and business opportunities are few. Many people have tried to make a living with drugs and gang activities. For a while Winton did not have a good reputation and nobody would move there if they had any other options.

But things are changing. This small town is waking up to its potential, in part because people started to come together, discover what they care about, and then act upon it. Charles always had a heart for senior citizens, so when he noticed an older man looking frail and ill, he found out that he had cancer and that his small, old home did not have glass in all the windows. In the winter that can become a problem, even in the central valley. So Charles brought some neighbors together! A glass business donated leftover single plane glass. There was a person who knew how to put glass in safely. There were a couple of handymen who were out of work who helped with the process. There were the tools that needed to be borrowed from someone. All of this was coordinated and organized by community members. It took a couple of weeks but it got done. "I can't believe we did this all by ourselves! It helped the handymen feel like they had something to give and did not just need a food handout. It gave purpose to the senior and he did not feel isolated any longer. It helped all of us to see what we can accomplish."

Yes, we could have called on a church in the nearby bigger towns. Yes, we could have pleaded with a business to step in. It would have repaired the windows but it would not have repaired the souls of the people involved.

As a result of this, the home owner felt valued and after he got healthier he helped some other seniors with landscaping. The business's good stewardship of its resources ended up earning them some good publicity in the process. The unemployed handymen did not just receive a handout when they came to our community center- they earned it with hard work! This story is not just an isolated incident. Many times Charles has looked back and said, "We did that.... what else can we do?"

We are bringing people together to become catalysts for change. We do not bring in outside resources until all internal options have been exhausted, because handouts will most often bring more heartache into the lives of people. When people have limited income they often rely on outside resources for Christmas gifts and school supplies; they are at the mercy of outsiders to provide for their children. How many fathers have hidden in the back room of their homes when outsiders brought presents for their children at Christmas?

There is a beautiful story where Jesus is spending the day preaching and teaching to a large group of men, women, and children. Late in the day his disciples noticed that the listeners must be very hungry and they go to Jesus. Jesus asks them, "What do you have?" He is inviting the larger community to be part of the miracle God is doing. He is inviting a little boy, who is willing to share his lunch, to be part of satisfying over 5,000 people.

Jesus could have done it himself; he could have just given them what they wanted and needed. But he did not! He let others be part of the solution.

Jesus often will start with questions, not because he does not know the answer but because he wants to remind us we have something to give. So a little boy gave his all and I always wondered what happened when he came home and his mom asked him how lunch was.

A city transforms when we know that everything in our community is of value, that the associations and businesses, the homeless and refugees, the hospitals and schools all have something to offer and when we know what we all can do. We can work together. We help community members know about the many resources that are already in the community and work together for the common good. *We leave a legacy when we recognize that God will multiply everyone's offerings, everyone's gifts, and create something much bigger than we can imagine.*

Discover the Gifts

Jack comes in to get peach juice from our community center. He is a homeless senior citizen who has fallen through the cracks of our system. He drinks way too much and years of abuse have left him shaking. On the wall of the center are sticky notes with people's gifts and skills and so we asked Jack "What are your gifts?" He mentioned that he can fix cars. So we wrote a bright yellow sticky note in big bold letters "Jack - car mechanic" and there it hung for weeks. But something amazing happened. Every time Jack came in to get his juice, the first thing he pointed to was the bright yellow sticky note. "That's me!" he would proclaim! Pointing out his inherent dignity gave him a small glimpse of hope and life.

When was the last time we asked the question "What gifts do you have?" We will often ask the question: "What do you do?" but not ask about skills, dreams, and passions. Our world is focused on accomplishments and so we "produce," but how often do we just be? Can we just be the people God has created us to be? How often do we get to see the things all around us and start discovering a much bigger picture?

Much of the time our work is mapping the assets around us. We map the things that are already present in a community. What does it smell like walking by the little hole-in-the-wall (probably illegal) bakery? Do we know that the owner is feeding several homeless neighbors every morning? What institutions or associations are present and what are they accomplishing? How are our schools run? Who are the teachers that spend so much time with the children and go the extra mile? What are the churches doing in town? How are they an asset to the community? What free, open space do we have for people to enjoy the outdoors?

We are using Asset Based Community Development principles so we map everything, but we see things through a certain lens. We don't focus on the negative - there are thousands of programs addressing the needs of people. Instead, we focus on the good things that are all around us. We see the graffiti on the wall as an artist waiting to be discovered. We see the drug dealer as a business entrepreneur; we see the homeless as a car mechanic; we see the associations as partners in making the community a better place; we see the churches as anchors for good and the agencies as places of resources for all. *A city transformed by Christ looks for possibilities and not problems. We respond, rather than react. We work in coordination with the community.*

Prevailing Hope

I am sitting at a table with Anne, one of our community members, processing a major confrontation that happened. She remarks she does not feel good enough to go to church or come to God. She mentions anger outbreaks and other questionable behaviors. She talks about her attempts to be "good enough." So I share with Anne about God's grace and mercy, and we talk about Christ's redemption and God's promise that he will remember our sins no more. I see a little glimpse of hope in her eyes, a little break that can turn her life around.

Proverbs 13:12 says: "Hope deferred makes a heart sick, but a longing fulfilled is a tree of life."

There is the hope deferred of not ever being good enough, or never moving out of a bad neighborhood, or never getting a better job or not seeing your child graduate. There is the hope deferred of having only the bare necessities in life, little healthy food on the table, clothing that makes people stare at you. But longing begins to be fulfilled when people realize the resources already in their hands. Asset Based Community Development helps people rewrite their story and look for the good around them and within them. But that means we have to build community. We have to be willing to enter into deep and difficult relationships, we have to be honest and vulnerable and come together to learn from each other.

This conversation did not happen in a vacuum. It took years of relationship to build trust, years to help this person see her value as a human being.

When we work with under-resourced neighborhoods we are not only addressing the socio-economic struggles the communities face but also the emotional and spiritual needs. People who have grown up in perpetual poverty are very resilient and have amazing non-formal educational skills, but they will often lack access to outside resources and access to role models who live in different circumstances.

When we first entered the community, we spent a lot of time praying and asking God to give us eyes to see what He sees. We asked for open doors, people of peace, and an invitation to work with a community.

Yes, we see the struggles the people are facing, the constant stress of dealing with lack of employment, lack of transportation, and little access to resources. Yes, we see the mental model of poverty that has been created through years of living in poverty. But we also see hope. We see people who want to see the world differently, who want to grow, engage, change, and move forward.

A few weeks after my "hope" conversation, the same person mentioned in a group setting that she is interested in going to college to further her education. It was a beautiful picture to see others coming alongside her, giving her advice, and sharing resources. There is hope in the community and it often comes in unexpected ways.

Hope was deferred for me as well, as the outsider. These conversations started five years after we entered the community. Five long years of building relationships, and praying for the community, five years of hope deferred. But then in two little glimpses I get to see longing fulfilled or, as Petersen puts it, "a sudden break that can turn life around" (Prov 13:12, *The Message*).

As we work with community members and bring them together to use the gifts and skills that they have to help each other, it is never about our timing but always their timing. It is about creating spaces where people can come together, learn from each other, see something new and different in the world around them, and start having a glimmer of hope for a better life. They can discover a life where they recognize that because of Christ, they don't have to be "good enough" on their own, and they can make changes to see something beautiful happening in their neighborhoods.

A city transforms when there is hope, a vision, a dream for the individual and the neighborhood, and a common vision for the whole town.

You might have heard the aphorism, "Please don't judge a person's story based on the page you walk into." At LifeLine we have a saying that "Everyone no matter how rich has a need. Everyone no matter how poor has a gift. That is why we build and celebrate community." We recognize that each of us has a story, a background we don't know about, a history that is often hidden (and sometimes unknown even to ourselves). So we don't judge people but we bring hope to seemingly hopeless situations. *In Christ-centered transformation we together discover God's prevailing hope.*

Caring Enough to Act

Jesus had a special love for children; he made time for them, protected them, and asked us to become more like them. So no wonder some of the community's focus is on their children. A few years ago several parents in Winton got together to talk about the long hot summer months that the children were out of school with nothing to do. They decided to do "Kids' Time," a two to three hour program several days a week with activities at the community center. It was a beautiful sight to see! Some parents made snacks, others prepared the crafts and science projects, others pulled out books to read. Young people shared their skills and earned their graduation service cords through their community work. Up to 30 children would come to the center for a few hours, read, learn, have fun, and play in the water, all in a safe environment for where they could forget the struggles of life.

All of it was organized by parents who cared enough to act, parents who may not hold a job, may have a drug addiction, and may be fighting their own demons, as well as young people who would otherwise get themselves into trouble. It was made possible by people who love Jesus and people who have never heard his name before.

The children had "homework;" math, reading, and social skills, all so they would be ready for the school year and not fall behind. A church provided backpacks for the children filled with supplies and the children earned their backpacks by completing their assignments. No handouts here!

My role was to ask questions, to ensure safety (such as with background checks), and to coach around age-appropriate games and skill building exercises. I coached on group dynamics and team interaction. We talked about values and strength-based collaboration. They partnered with the local library so the kids could get their own cards and learn to how to visit the library.

In the end, the children were enriched because parents cared enough to act. When they saw hurting children, they prayed for and with them, because that is what Jesus would have done. When they met parents and entered into deep conversations they shared resources that might help them along the way.

Paul tells Timothy: "You have often heard me teach. Now I want you to tell these same things to followers who can be trusted to tell others" (2 Tim 2:2). We need to teach others who then teach others.

The story of Kid's Time has expanded. There is now a monthly reading club for kids to develop a love of reading and a game night for children to play board games, learn new social skills, practice cognitive reasoning, and have fun. Some of the kids are now teenagers and help with graffiti abatement and give back to the community, learning leadership skills and work ethic. *We are bringing hope to the city when we empower people with the skills they need to accomplish their dreams. We are helping leave a legacy when we pass on what we know.*

Never do for people what they can do for themselves

"We want to start a Bible study at your center," a local church requested. At first I was delighted. YES! A church wants to invest in its own community! But as I learned more and I heard more about their vision I recognized this was not for the sake of the community members, but really for the sake of church growth. I often have to remind well-meaning Christ-followers that it is never about church growth but about kingdom growth. Just yesterday I again heard a person mention he has to "sit through 20 minutes of preaching" to get his box of food to care for his family. God's kingdom advances when word and deed are combined, when people connect with each other, when we learn to hear each other's stories, and when we support each other during our times of struggle. kingdom growth happens when I am vulnerable enough to let people enter into my struggle and they see my trust in God.

Empowering people means we step back and wait until they are ready to hear, engage, and learn. That does not mean I am silent about my faith, but it means I don't preach at people. I earn the right to be heard. People are hungry for a deep relationship with God, but abuse, neglect, and a wrong picture of God's grace and mercy have left them with a bitter taste. So we live out our faith very openly but don't expect people to follow unless God has drawn them into it.

But this is just one of the areas we want to change. There are many others: food giveaways, Christmas toy drives, handouts to the homeless, programs that have too many strings attached. Our quick fixes often can be more detrimental to our neighbors than we imagine. Toy drives during Christmas are a good way to give back, but they often have unintended consequences. When the children receive a trash bag full of toys, they often don't value what they have received, and it creates a dependency and undermines the dignity of parents who cannot compete with it. We have changed that model a bit. We still receive donated toys, but we ensure they are of high quality and are family-building. We then create a Christmas Store and invite parents to shop for their children and only pay 20% of the value of the gift (so a $20 toy will cost them $4). Then the parents are invited to wrap the gifts and take them home for their children. This gives value to parents as they provide for their children, it honors the parents by letting them choose the toys their children would enjoy, and it helps the children see their parents as providers. The Christmas Store is organized by community members who know their neighbors and know how to engage with them. This reflects what John McKnight discovered,

> I knew from being a neighborhood organizer that you could never change people or neighborhoods with the basic proposition that what we need to do is fix them," he said. "What made for change was communities that believed they had capacities, skills, abilities and could create power when they came together in a community.

We don't start programs. We don't bring in resources. We don't "fix" things. We wait until community members are at a point of discovering what they feel would benefit them and ask for help from the outside.

By the way, there is a vibrant Bible study going on at the community center. A group of women under Rose's leadership started out just getting together and working on a crafts project together while listening to a Bible study teaching video. They discussed having a more formal study and connected with a pastor they knew and asked if he would be willing to come and help them study the Bible and pray together. Every Wednesday evening a small group of people comes together, learns about God, and prays for their community. *We lead by stepping back. We share our faith in the context of growing relationships and respond when people are ready to take the next step.*

Creating Synergy by Working in Collaboration

Years ago a community member named David returned to Winton after being the first college graduate in his family. He could not find a job and was looking for opportunities to serve the local community. We observed that many of the local community members did not know they can file for their tax return, even if they are on a very limited income, so we partner with the IRS through the VITA (Volunteer Income Tax Assistance) Program. David got trained to assist low-income families with their free tax preparation. A small donation from an individual provided a stipend for him and supplies came through a local church and a small grant. In the first year many people had their taxes done for the first time and received refunds that helped them cover some of their expenses.

The second year, we partnered with a local organization and David was able to train some other volunteers to help with it. Last year, he oversaw the training for a dozen people and in the local area of Winton over $200,000 came back into the local economy in tax refunds because of him. He used his gifts, partnered with other agencies, empowered other volunteers, and helped the whole community. All this started with one a young man not being able to find a job!

Incidentally he now works two jobs, one of them as an adjunct professor at a local college. Some of the skills he learned at our community center are coming in handy now that he is teaching. *We lead by stepping back. We share our faith in the context of growing relationships and respond when people are ready to take the next step.*

Shalom in the Community

Many times we quote Jeremiah 29:11 as one of our favorite verses: "For I know the plans I have for you," declares the Lord, "Plans to prosper you and not to harm you, plans to give you a hope and a future."

This is a beautiful promise of God that he will direct us and care for us. But often we forget to read the context of this Scripture. It is part of a letter to the exiled, families who have been taken to another country and are living away from their beloved home. They had every right to be angry and frustrated and unloving to their captors. But what the letter states is against human nature:

"This is what the Lord Almighty says...build houses and settle down, plant gardens... seek the peace (Shalom) and prosperity of the city to which I have carried you into exile. Pray to the Lord for it, because if it prospers, you too will prosper" (Jer 29:1–7).

Shalom means completeness, wholeness, health, peace, welfare, safety, soundness, tranquility, prosperity, perfectness, fullness, rest, harmony, and the absence of agitation or discord. We are called to usher in the shalom of God into our communities, the places we live, the cities we call home, the state that surrounds us. We are called to bring health, well-being and wholeness.

When we actively engage with the community things change. In Winton it came in the form of a garden.

As community members were coming together in Winton they recognized they are living in a food desert. They might be working the fields to bring in the abundant harvest, yet they did not have access to healthy fresh fruits and vegetables for their own families. So we started dreaming together.

Things began to happen! Through a partnership with the Health Department we had some funds to start a community garden. A local business owner let us use an open piece of land and his water. Jacob, Tina, and Fred led the community members to work together and they started preparing the ground, building the raised beds, and planting the initial crop. It was a delight to watch. People from all walks of life are working together to create something beautiful. Some neighbors brought seeds, others gave their expertise, others decorated, some came early in the morning to water the garden and yet others pluck the nasty bugs off the tomato leaves.

There are no barriers; the garden is out in the open and anybody can come and work at it. There are no boundaries; we have rich and poor, homeless and homeowners, men and women from every walk of life coming together to work the ground and create something beautiful. In a town where graffiti and vandalism is prevalent, this garden has stood out as a sign of shalom -a place of well-being and safety, a place where there is no discord but instead rest and harmony.

As community members continue to dream they are envisioning benches where people can sit and rest, and they want to replicate it in other parts of their community. They enjoy the journey and the harvest. *We lead by stepping back. We share our faith in the context of growing relationships and respond when people are ready to take the next step.*

Moving Forward

> Every single person has capabilities, abilities and gifts. Living a good life depends on whether those capabilities can be used, abilities expressed and gifts given. If they are, the person will be valued, feel powerful and well-connected to the people around them. And the community around the person will be more powerful because of the contribution the person is making (John P. Kretzmann and John L. McKnight)

A majority of people living in Winton are Latino, many of them undocumented residents who live in the shadow of that stigma. You can pick them out. Their heads are often downcast. They live in the shadows, always staying quietly behind, overlooked and under-appreciated. We benefit from their hard labor in the fields that bring us fresh fruits and vegetables, but otherwise we don't see them. Yet each one of them has an amazing story. Each one has gifts and skills and much informal education. They are a huge asset to our community and yet we don't often communicate. There are not only the language and cultural barriers but also the fear of me (the white woman) turning them in.

For years I thought we should have an English-Spanish conversation class, a place where English speakers can learn Spanish and Spanish folks could learn English... so I prayed and waited for the right time. But I kept it mostly to myself and just waited for people to talk about it.

Then one day at a community meeting one of our bilingual parents, Veronica, talked about the idea of a conversation class. It would be a place where there is not a "student-teacher" role distinction but where both would learn from each other. And so they got started. Initially Jill and I joined them but we realized soon that we were becoming a hindrance. Our presence obligated the community members to refer to us as teachers and dampened some of the deep conversation they could have without us there.

They met for several months, learned from each other, celebrated birthdays together, and experienced life. People walked away more confident to communicate in another language and started talking about working together on their driver's licenses and immigration issues. They exchanged their knowledge with each other and learned from each other. They went to First Communion together and learned about different faith expressions.

Cultural, socio-economic, religious, and ethnic barriers can take a lot of time to overcome. It is often better to lead by stepping back and coaching individuals who then become our cultural translators. We do not need to be at the center of everything. We can lead by stepping back.

To leave a legacy that is Christ-centered we need to empower more and instruct less.

This is All You Know

In our community we have a saying: "If this is all you know, then this is all you know." People who live under the daily stress of poverty often do not think they have a voice that needs to be heard. They may have never spoken up for their rights. They don't know some of the rights they have.

As the people of Winton began to envision better outcomes, they recognized they need to be part of the larger political landscape. We started talking about the political processes of government, of those who wield power and privilege and how to engage in good and healthy conversations and become politically active. In a place of isolation, individuals started going to meetings of other associations and groups. They would learn what other community members were doing and recognize that they were not the only ones making positive changes in Winton. They started to partner with other groups on events and share resources. They learned to celebrate the work of others and not see it as competition. They learned to advocate for themselves.

Vero, a community organizer who would not have looked into your eyes two years ago, went before a group of health officials to share about the work on the community garden. She was shaking in fear and stepped outside before speaking to gather her courage, because she did not think she could do it. But she did and when we reflect on it today she stands up taller and more confident than before.

Expanding the horizons of people who have lived in poverty, helping them to find their voice again, and helping them to seek not only mercy but justice is an important part of leaving a legacy for a city. The Bible calls us to advocate for people who have been treated unjustly.

Vero is no longer working with us, but I know that she is more confident in her ability to stand up for herself and her family. She has even been offered a job as a translator. *Our work in city transformation included helping people find justice in a world that often feels unjust towards marginalized people.*

With Liberty and Justice for All

As I am writing this, a dear friend and community connector is lying the hospital with a major medical issue that might cost his life. I wonder if he is getting the same care that I would have gotten under similar circumstances. This young African American man grew up in a world that taught him early on that he needs to keep his head down and not draw any attention to himself. I have seen it numerous times; when injustices happened to him, he would just take it and not rock the boat. When he was questioned why he had "white kids" with him while at a community event, he just kept his mouth shut and showed them the permissions slips from the parents.

As we debriefed these incidents I wanted to fight for him, stand up for him, and make things right. But I don't want to be another white person in charge who comes to his rescue. Instead, I'd rather empower him with tools and resources to learn to stand strong and use his God-given talents to make a difference.

We have come a long way over the last 50 years on the issue of justice and equity, but there is so much to be done.

Bob Linthicum says "Poverty is not so much the absence of goods as it is the absence of power, the capability of being able to change one's situation" (Linthicum, 1991, 1). Only when we give power and capacity for people to change will they be able to stand up for themselves and discover their God-given rights and dignity.

Over the years, I have seen this young man grow stronger and taller, willing to stand up for things that are right, for others and for him personally. *What would Christ do today to show evidence of a transformed city? He would stand up for the voiceless, protect the undefended and care for those who cannot care for themselves. We can do this by empowering people.*

Who Are You?

In the book *When Helping Hurts,* Steve Corbett says: "Until we embrace our mutual brokenness, our work with low-income people is likely to do more harm than good" (Corbett and Fikkert, 2014, 61). I sometimes unintentionally reduce poor people to objects that I use to fulfill my own need to accomplish something. I am not okay, and you are not okay. But Jesus can fix us both.

Living in poverty means that often you don't believe you are of value and nobody cares about a small, unincorporated town like Winton. Winton has an amazing county supervisor and she comes regularly to visit Winton. Often she has to reintroduce herself and share who she is, but now people are more informed of the political framework they are living in and know that she can make things happen! The community center also has a monthly visit from our district representative for our State Senator and we have wonderful conversations about how the wheels of government move. Winton had visits from the Health Department and even the staff of the Centers for Disease Control and Prevention and the community members got to show off their garden. All this breaks down the barriers of "them vs us" and assists community members in gaining knowledge and access to resources they never knew existed.

Last week we had our after-Christmas party at our home. Twenty community members from our various centers came to join us and enjoy homemade pizza. We all started out with the basic dough but then every person got to create his or her own pizza. Some are meat lovers and that was all you could see on the pizza. Others liked it plain. Everyone had her own creation. We baked it in shifts and shared with each other. As I was reflecting on it I was reminded that we are all coming from the same Creator, but each of us has different gifts, skills, and abilities and we are put together differently. God intended it that way: none alike, all unique, all with different stories. But when we come together we can create something beautiful. There is a proverb attributed to Lao Tzu that reflects our work well:

> *Go to the people*
> *Live among them*
> *Learn from them*
> *Love them*
> *Start with what they know*
> *Build on what they have*
> *But of the best leaders*
> *When their task is done*
> *The people will remark*
> *"We have done it ourselves."*

In the work we are doing we are using Asset Based Community Development principles and practices. We want to amplify the community voice and step back in our leadership. The basic steps are simple:

1. We walk and pray. We really need to prepare our own hearts to enter a community. Too many times over the years we have seen groups coming in with agendas that serve their own purposes. As we walk and pray we see God's heart, we see the good in the community, and we develop a love for the community.

2. We listen and listen some more. We get to know people, hear their stories, learn from them, and experience what their lives are like. We discover the gifts and skills of the community members and start creating an asset map.

3. We have conversations around a common vision. We discover what people care about and what they want to see changed.

4. We map all the assets in the community: the people, the associations, the organizations, the institutions, and the physical spaces. We want transparency and let people see all the resources that are already present.

5. We work in collaborative efforts around things that the community wants to change by creating healthy, equal relationships between people and organizations.

6. We empower people by bringing in outside resources and knowledge they cannot provide for themselves.

7. We work together towards more equitable solutions for everyone.

We celebrate all successes, big and small, and look for new ways to work together to bring the Shalom of God into the community.

After eight years of working in Winton we see some system changes happening. Here are just a few:

- More community members have voices on boards that determine the future of their community.

239

- A Winton Community Plan is being developed that is involving more community members as part of the decision.
- Gang activities and graffiti have gone down.
- Nonprofits and organizations are collaborating more.
- More people are culturally aware and appreciative.
- The Health Department is helping the community have access to healthier options as determined by community members.
- Relationships between the supportive institutions (health, law enforcement, schools) is getting stronger.
- It is a safer environment for young people.

We do not claim that we can take direct credit for any of this, but by bringing community members together and helping them have a voice we did our part to "Put Winton on the map for something good."

As we think about long-term solutions and Christ-centered city transformation, we need to learn to see the amazing gifts and skills of people who live in the neighborhoods. Seeing people as created by God, redeemed by grace, and restored towards Shalom leaves us all with a deep hope and amazed by God's gracious power to transform.

Works Cited

Corbett, Steve & Brian Fikkert, (2014). *When Helping Hurts*. Chicago, IL: Moody Publishers.

The Holy Bible, (1995). Contemporary English Version. New York: American Bible Society.

The Holy Bible, (2013). New International Version. Grand Rapids: Zondervan House.

Lao Tzu, Tao Te Ching, Chinese Proverb *Go to the People*

Linthicum, Bob, (1991). *Empowering the Poor*. Monrovia, CA: Missions Advanced Research,

McKnight, John and Peter Block, (2012). *The Abundant Community*. Oakland, CA: Berrett-Koehler Publishers.

John McKnight: Low-income Communities are not Needy -- They Have Assets. (2015, January 13). *Faith and Leadership,* retrieved from https://www.faithandleadership.com/john-mcknight-low-income-communities-are-not-needy-they-have-assets

Perkins, John (1976). *Let Justice Roll Down*, Ventura, CA.: Regal Books.

Petersen, Eugene, *The Message,* Colorado Springs: NavPress, 2009

Chapter Eight

A Church OF and FOR the Community: A Case Study of On Ramps Covenant Church

Phil and Rici Skei

(Phil), Neighborhood Revitalization Manager, City of Fresno

(Rici and Phil) Co-Pastors Onramps Covenant Church

As God's people, we are far more powerful than we think we are. We can make a profound difference in our neighborhoods, communities, and cities – far greater than we believe we can.

Robert Linthicum

It was a typical Sunday morning. We were running late as usual – grabbing a quick bite on the run, slipping on high heels, forming the last knot in the tie, running back upstairs to grab our Bibles. We could NOT be late for church. So you understand our frustration when we tell you we didn't have any time to waste on a conversation with a neighbor who was obviously distraught, broken, needing a listening ear, and maybe needing a few dollars. We looked at him and said something that would haunt us to this day, words that ended up being a catalyst for a major paradigm shift concerning how we view the church. We told him, "Wait! We are running late for church and we'll talk to you when we get back!" I know, you're shaking your head in disbelief. Yes, it's hard to admit, but we LEFT church to go to church. We missed an opportunity to BE the church because we were rushing to get to church.

It was a typical Sunday morning, but the car ride to church was not. It was filled with embarrassment. We bombarded God with questions about what the church is really about. Was church really just about warming pews, putting on our finest suits, ties, and facades, shaking a few hands as we put money in the collection bin, hearing a few great songs and listening to a moderately-prepared sermon? Or was there more? If there was more, what was our specific role in it all? If there was more, and God revealed our particular role in it all, would our neighbors have equal access to this church, including the neighbor we abandoned in our front yard with tears in his eyes? Would it include our neighbors struggling with adequate housing for their five children? Could it include our neighbor who needs assistance paying for her court-appointed drug rehabilitation program?

Haven't we *all* dreamed this dream? It is the one we share in our small groups and among our friends. It is that the church would be more than just a gathering place, but a *mission*. This is the dream that causes our hearts to leap! It is why we are drawn to the opening scenes of the Acts of the Apostles, but is also why we avoid reading them. We live in the tension of allowing ours hearts to hope for a church that would be as vibrant as the early church while having witnessed generations of them start out with great promise only to find themselves susceptible to the lure of the dominant model.

This chapter is a case study of a church that is still holding onto that hope and being influenced by that dream, and doing so by placing its mission in the center of its shared life –by *tying a geography to its identity*. On Ramps Covenant Church is certainly no "model" and we can't claim that we won't someday be assimilated into the same dominant model as others who have gone before us. The truth is we aren't trying to be a model, but we do feel this strong sense of call toward a framework that has emerged out of postmodernity and is what we believe to be an expression of God's current reformation of the Church.

And as we are pursuing this "way of being" we are finding that it deeply resonates with a generation that has the same dream we do. Our prayer is that others will join us in living out this dream - not just in being a church that is *in* and *to* the community, but in becoming a church that is *of* and *for* the community.

Our community sits in a context, and that context is important. In order to understand the story of On Ramps you have to understand the emerging story of Fresno, California. In 2006 the Brookings Institute published a study evaluating the concentrated poverty of major cities throughout the United States (Berube and Katz, 2005). This study came on the heels of Hurricane Katrina and sought to explore the adverse impact the failed levy had upon poor people in New Orleans. The theory was that the reason a single levy failing impacted so many poor people was due to a concentration of poor people living in the same communities. In other words, social biases influencing city policy and planning can force poor people to live in particular areas of the city, and to live together, thus creating a poverty concentration in our cities. This kind of policy making and planning is contrary to what we know about how to build healthy cities through diverse neighborhoods. At the release of this study the Brookings Institute concluded that New Orleans indeed had a very high degree of concentrated poverty. In fact, they had the second-highest degree of concentrated poverty of any major city in the country - second only to Fresno.

Fresno had been at or near the top of other negative reports before - car theft and teen pregnancy to name two - but these were all circumstances that Fresno could explain by pointing our finger at the poor and "solve" by delivering more programs or providing police intervention. However, the issue of concentrated poverty was a different animal. This was the result of poor policy and governmental neglect, if

244

not the result of intentional governmental design, which felt eerily
familiar to times of legislated segregation and redlining. Finding out we
had the highest degree of concentrated poverty in the country shook our
city. We knew we were facing some challenges as a city, but we didn't
know how deep they were. This report was eye-opening to our elected
officials and to our communities. It demanded a radical shift in policy
and implementation, and called for new models of engagement to emerge

from within the community itself.

Concentrated Poverty Map - City of Fresno

It is out of this context that On Ramps Covenant Church emerged, a church in a city where 500 other churches already existed. For us it begged the question, how can our city struggle so terribly with poverty and at the same time have a church on nearly every block? Our conviction was not that the existing 500 churches were ineffective - it was just that their effectiveness was in areas that did not impact poverty. In other words, most of Fresno's churches are *in* and *to* neighborhoods throughout our city, which has resulted in them performing charitable activities, but not contributing to sustainable signs of resurrection. In birthing On Ramps, our commitment was not to form the 501st church in our city, but to join a very small aggregation of churches spread thinly throughout our city's 22 highest-poverty neighborhoods who are *of* and *for* these communities. It is a different paradigm, one that would exhibit a different type of relationship between the church and its surrounding community.

On Ramps Covenant Church is an Evangelical Covenant Church plant of the Pacific Southwest Conference. We are a Jesus-following, multi-ethnic, multi-class, multi-cultural, multi-generational church that is pursuing reconciliation. This ethos has propelled us to pioneer some work in our city that we believe is somewhat unique. For On Ramps, some expressions of this unique ethos are:

Street Parishes – Staying connected to the community can be a challenge over time. It is far too easy for a church that is *of* and *for* the community to lose its connection to the neighborhood simply as a result of working to support existing structures and responding to congregational needs. This, along with the classic challenge of facilitating deeper community within the congregation, can be overwhelming. On Ramps chose to develop a structure that would address both of these challenges. We call this structure a "Street Parish." Street Parishes are our version of small groups that gather monthly and convene those that live on the neighborhood street the parish is named after (i.e. Poplar Street Parish or Yosemite Street Parish). Those who are part of the congregation but don't live in the church's parish neighborhood are welcome to choose any street parish they wish to join. Street Parishes deepen community and are tasked with helping the church become aware of crisis events or moments of celebration on their street, and leading us in a loving response.

Community Ministry Team – It is still far too easy for a multi-class, multi-ethnic church to become mono-class and mono-ethnic even despite the many creative structures it establishes. Therefore, On Ramps has empowered key residents within our geography to serve on our Community Ministry Team whose responsibility it is to serve as "brokers" to the community. They support Street Parish conveners when they feel ill-equipped to respond to a neighborhood event, have flexibility to lead various mustard-seed activities, and help us stay current with regard to what is happening in the neighborhood.

Social Enterprises – A church that is *of* and *for* its community will likely enter into relationship with people needing work and income. Many churches respond by making one-time monetary donations to families, but On Ramps has chosen to develop social enterprise businesses that employ people who are "unemployed, underemployed, and unemployable" (On Ramps Economic Development Corporation, 2016). We have launched two social enterprises already, Say Hello Advertising and Valley Edible Landscapes.

"Come and Dine" – The holidays are a time of great need in so many communities each year. Many of us have participated in food giveaways and toy giveaways. On Ramps, in an effort to be *of* and *for* the

community, decided to approach the need for food and community on Thanksgiving differently. Years ago we created "Come and Dine," a Thanksgiving luncheon at our neighborhood park. This luncheon has some of the finest live entertainment in the city, and incredible home-cooked meals for each of the 45 tables. Each year we partner with other neighborhood churches to find families within their congregations that are willing to host a table. "Hosting" means they will cook a common, predetermined menu for their table and decorate it. Hosting also means that you sit down at your table of eight and eat alongside anyone who joins you. This approach moves us away from doing things *to* the neighborhood because we cultivate "family" around each table every year. Members of the community have begun to look for certain table hosts year after year because the relationships that are being established are so important. Indeed, they are becoming "family."

Choosing to be Bivocational – "Bivocational" is a fancy term for saying "you have two jobs." It is our conviction as a church *of* and *for* our community that many of our staff be bivocational, including at least one of our co-pastors. This decision affects the flexibility of our leadership team and staff team but helps us remain connected to the experience of our parish members. It follows the wisdom of never making decisions without having people who will be affected by the decision at the table. Therefore, decisions that we make concerning gathering structures or setting meeting times that affect working members of our parish are being made by various volunteer and bivocational staff, including one of our co-pastors! This enables the church to allocate more resources to our mission (rather than staff) and pay more people to commit hours to this mission through smaller staff assignments. Additionally, this conviction has enabled our church to access additional mission-related resources through the city of Fresno because our bivocational co-pastor works as their Neighborhood Revitalization Manager directing the work of rebuilding poor neighborhoods (see section in this chapter on "Vision 22").

Philosophical/Theological Foundation

The "On Ramps way" has been deeply influenced by the philosophies and theology articulated by the Christian Community Development Association (CCDA) and Leadership Foundations (LF) movements. It is our opinion as pastors that these two movements bring significant gifts that are essential to absorb if you desire to make the fundamental shift from being a church *in* and *to* the community, to becoming a church that is *of* and *for* the community in which you serve. We have taken the biblical teaching of these two movements, and expressed the framework by which On Ramps lives, in a term we have coined: the "Contemporancient Church."

This term is achieved from conflating the words "contemporary" and "ancient" as an expression of a generation of the corporate Church that yearns to hold together the ancient expressions of our Christian faith with our contemporary expressions. The saying we often repeat is, "if it is from God, then we want it!" In other words, there is a sense among this generation that evangelicalism has become "thin," but also an acknowledgment that we are culturally bound by its influence. This generation is longing for something deeper, often that which has stood the test of time, that roots our faith and submerges us into the Person of God. Sadly, this longing is often not embraced within our evangelical circles because the ancient Christian expressions we are being drawn toward are unknown to modern evangelicalism - they are carnage left behind in the wake of Protestant protests over hundreds of years. And so we long for something that many of our churches are not interested in embracing but something that our souls need, and our generation's culture affirms, in order to live out the hope of the resurrection. It is amidst this tension that a "Contemporancient Church" has emerged that is embracing both the contemporary and the ancient in one faithful generation. The values of a church that locates itself amidst this generation can be expressed in the following terms:

Tension-Embracing: To become a church that is *of* the community means we are inviting a measure of diversity that can bring tension because we live in a diverse community. The fundamental posture of this type of church toward tension is to embrace it. It is commonly said that at On Ramps we "lean into the tension." This is a posture founded on our core belief that God is greater than anything that divides us, and our affirmation that we are "free in Christ" (Hawkinson et al., 2005, 18). The church understands its position as unique because its mission is centered around reconciliation. To this generation it means that the church must seek to hold together in relationship everything that has historically divided us because everything that makes us diverse comes from God. We do this by creating a culture of grace, not perfection, extending forgiveness toward ourselves and others, and by trusting that if we truly welcome people from our community and city into our structures and systems the Holy Spirit will hold it all together.

Parish-Minded: A church will never be *for* a place if it is not seen by others and if it does not see itself as *of* that place. Joseph was *of* Arimathea, Paul was *of* Tarsus, Jesus was *of* Nazareth. To be *of* a place you must define the place, connect yourself with that place, and never exercise your privilege to disassociate yourself from that place. Reid Carpenter, founder of Leadership Foundations, would often travel to cities and challenge his audience with the question, "You live in your city, but does your city live in you?" He would then implore his audience to make a commitment to their city by purchasing their grave plots there. While Reid invited people to commit to their city, a church *of* its community and *for* its community must make a commitment to a more specific, narrowly defined geography that it will commit to serve. When there is tragedy in this community, the church will respond. When there is something to celebrate, the church will wave its flags. Where there is need, the church will do its best to meet it. Where there is hope, the church will work to spread it. This geography will become its "parish" and will be the place where the church will use its various resources, gifts, and talents to pursue God's kingdom vision of shalom.

Partnership-Oriented: Being a tension-embracing, parish-minded church means that you have already embodied a posture that openly seeks partnership. Your parish is too large, its needs are too great, and the expertise required is too vast for your church to pursue God's vision of shalom there alone. In fact, we believe this is by design. God gave us a vision too big for us to achieve without partnering with the rest of the body. Leadership Foundations challenges us to seek the spiritual and social renewal of our cities by partnering with people of faith and good will (Hillis, 2015, xi). is requires the church to confront its bias toward the doctrine of "special grace" and its tendency to ignore that God has also granted our world a more "common grace" (Keller, 2005). The implications of a more generous theological posture is that your church will communicate to its community and city that it is open to partnering with anyone who is willing to do anything that will move the community closer to its own vision. Simply stated, if you are willing to help in the ways in which the community has asked, then we are willing to partner with you until we see God's kingdom fully manifested in our parish. This preparedness to partner is a strong statement that the church is not just *in* the community but it is unapologetically *for* its community. One example of this posture is the partnership On Ramps established with the City of Fresno, Tree Fresno, and the Lowell Neighborhood Association to re-plant street trees along one of our parish's major streets. The vision originated with the neighborhood association who expressed their grief over the dozens of street trees that had been stolen, had died, or had been run over by vehicles throughout the years and never replaced. They needed a partner to take the lead on navigating the planting process with the City of Fresno, and they needed a source for new trees. On Ramps agreed to take the lead on this project and immediately contacted Tree Fresno, one of our local environmental advocacy organizations who agreed to donate what they could and get us discounts on materials they couldn't. With replacement trees firmly secured On Ramps approached the city to learn what barriers may exist to re-planting these trees. This led to the creation of an entire tree and irrigation inventory of the street, coordination with the city's arborist for the planting of proper species in appropriate locations, and a new partnership with a local landscaping company that would cut and remove concrete in locations where we needed new tree wells! Some of these people are Christian, but none of them worked for Christian organizations. However, none of this was ever a barrier to our partnership because our sole focus was upon the redemption of our parish, which made these partnerships and this planting project possible! The result of this posture is the beautification of a street travelled by thousands of people each week who better understand that God loves this neighborhood and that his Spirit is actively establishing his kingdom here!

Mission-Driven: At the beginning of every meeting we read this mission statement aloud: *"On Ramps Covenant Church exists to be a healing community healing its community."* It is posted prominently in our chapel. It is repeated in conversations and in our gatherings by many people over time. It is never neglected. Why? Because most churches are comprised of people who are accustomed to satisfying their own needs. In Scripture we are introduced to this self-serving life in Revelation 12 and Genesis 3 when Lucifer sought to be worshipped, was evicted from Heaven, and then invited Eve and Adam to become the subject of worship themselves. He told Eve, "You will be like God." And so they ate the fruit they were forbidden to eat by God, and received their own eviction notices from the garden God had prepared for them. If we are not disciplined in reminding ourselves that we exist not to fulfill our own mission but to fulfill a mission that God has given us, then we will too easily fall into the trap of being engaged in activity that serves our own self-justifiable needs. To be clear, the church really doesn't have a mission - God's mission has a church. Everything we are begins with God, not ourselves. And so to become a church that is *for* its community, the church must build God's mission into all of its structures in order to "renew the minds" of those of us who have a propensity to co-opt everything we do for our own glory. To be driven by the *Missio Dei* (mission of God) is to accept God's invitation for our own redemption and to radically alter our trajectory toward ourselves and become a people that does not just gather *in* a community but gathers *for* the sake of the community. The question we ask is, "In what ways does the well-being of the community affect the well-being of the church?" When there is a shooting in the neighborhood, do we move our worship gathering to the place where the violence occurred? When someone moves into the community do we welcome them? Do we consistently track the crime stats for our community and pray for breakthrough as a church? When one of the youth in the community excels athletically does the church celebrate? The mission God created the church to pursue isn't simply concerned with church members but is always inclusive of community members. It is for this reason that the church will not be satisfied until the mission is fulfilled among the entire parish community, and this is how the church comes to understand who it is and why it exists.

Gift-Valuing: When a church makes a commitment to participate in the transformation of its community, it has embraced a mission that is larger than the pastor's preaching and the choir's singing gifts can carry them. Therefore, developing a culture that seeks to identify, affirm, and release the gifts of each member of the church is essential. To accomplish the vision of the church, the church must release the gifts of evangelism, art, strategy, introversion, healing, construction, prophecy, administration, minstrels, and so many more. God has given everyone gifts! Therefore, the pursuit of the mission of the church is not the task of a small group but of all. The community needs these gifts to be released, and the carriers of these gifts need to release them - for the healing of others, as well as for their own healing. For On Ramps this has meant that "team" is a fundamental structure for everything we do. Teams naturally deepen our relationships with one another, enable us to discover the gifts of God in others, and create space for those gifts to be activated. On Ramps has a team that plans our worship gatherings every Saturday, a team that makes decisions about financial assistance requests from the community, a team that leads our youth ministry, and so many more.

Burden-Bearing: The church is about people. It has always been about people. It *is* a people. If a deep love for each other and the community is not the driving force for the church's community engagement, then the fate of the ministry has been sealed. Apart from the holy compassion that Jesus had for the hungry crowds that followed Him, the ministry of the church will inevitably fall into the traps like objectification, paternalism, and exploitation as they seek to be in a transformational relationship with the community. In contrast, if the culture of the church encourages public confession, sharing meals, and prayer ministry, among other things, then bearing the burdens of one another will translate into shouldering the burden of an entire community. For example, our neighbor, Connie was seven months pregnant with her fifth child when she left her physically abusive husband. Immediately, some of the younger men in the church provided mentorship for her older children while the women in the church hosted a baby shower so her soon-to-be-born daughter had the essentials. Relationships matter and transparency is important. One of the ways On Ramps seeks to firmly engrain this into our culture is by creating spaces for conversations of depth each Tuesday and Saturday we gather. Being an intentionally multi-ethnic church, when devastating instances of racial injustice and violence are shown on television or social media, we don't ignore these tragedies. We don't continue with business as usual. We don't dismiss the pain and fear of others, even if we don't fully understand the systemic and individual reality of it all. Instead, we pause to reflect, lament, pray, and take action as a Body. We facilitate honest discussions, listen to one another, and pledge to speak up for those who are voiceless. In addition to conversations, we are always praying for one another during our gatherings, and when prayer needs become known throughout the week they are posted on our private Facebook group or passed along to the Elder Board Chair who sends a text message to other elders inviting them to pray and respond in other tangible ways.

Description of the Neighborhood

We've all had the experience of driving past a restaurant and immediately knowing what type of food it served simply by the aroma being released. We've all heard the melody of a song and have been able to place it in a specific musical genre. We've all experienced sheer joy just by seeing something pleasurable. Well, so it is with the Lowell neighborhood. It's difficult to explain, but it definitely has its own distinct smells, sounds, and sights. Lowell is somewhat like a really good movie - full of twists and turns, highs and lows, surprises and subtleties, and tragedies and triumphs. Like a movie that ultimately you cannot adequately describe, Lowell just has to be experienced in order to truly appreciate its depth and complexities.

The Lowell neighborhood is a very unique place. Once known as the "Devil's Triangle," this neighborhood is now known for its collaborative leaders and God-given mission. Comprised of 750 properties, 1,500 addresses, and 6,800 residents, its residents are 66% Latino (half of these are estimated to be undocumented), 15% White, 11% Asian, and 8% Black. Seventy-five percent of this community does not hold a high school diploma and the median income is just under $13,000 annually. This is On Ramps Covenant Church's "parish."

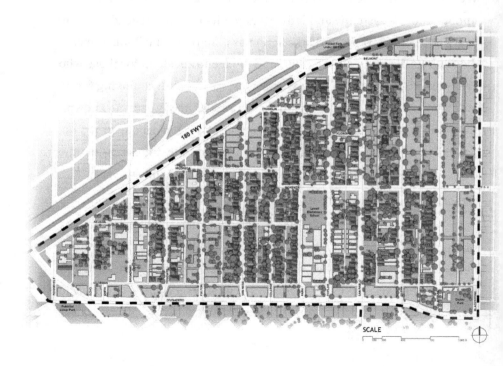

To be a church that is *of* and *for* its community, you must <u>know</u> your community. Jacob Huang's chapter on *Data in Service of Transformation* is helpful here. There are a number of things you can do to be introduced to your community. The most impersonal, important, way to get to know your community is by gathering statistics on subjects such as demographics, crime, income, and education. Statistics are valuable but they must be interpreted, which is why in your pursuit of learning your community you must also listen to the stories of people who live in your community. This happens by ensuring your church is regularly prayer walking its neighborhood, eating in neighborhood establishments, getting their vehicles repaired by local mechanics, and playing at the local park. As one final layer of information, a church that is *of* and *for* its community should encourage its membership to become part of neighborhood associations, join the boards of community organizations that directly serve your parish community, and serve on civic committees that shape policy and funding decisions for your neighborhood.

The Practicalities of Embracing Geography

"You can change the world!" It's a declaration that has become cliché. While some of us believe this declaration, others of us don't buy the rhetoric. Phil and I choose to believe another declaration; a third way, if you will. Yes, you can change the world (another way of saying it is "you can make a difference"), as long as you are committed - committed to a people, committed to a place, committed to a purpose. In 2006, our family chose to commit ourselves to a place. In 2011, our church chose to commit its vision, mission, and values to this same place.

Commitment to a place, or embracing geography, has done several things. First, it has allowed ministry, in all of its complexities, to be a bit more bite-sized. Let me put it this way: our family observes "Family Night" every Wednesday and often we order pizza to celebrate the night (and because, quite frankly, this mama doesn't feel like cooking!). I always say, there is a reason why pizzas are cut in slices: so you can eat one piece at a time. Being committed to a place, in our case the Lowell Neighborhood, has allowed us to savor the pizza (that is, Fresno) one slice at a time. It has allowed us to not feel so overwhelmed by the demands of all of the issues that currently trouble our city, and yet commit to addressing these issues on a very local, "bite-sized" level.

Have you ever watched the concluding portion of a movie and suddenly the words, "To be continued..." appeared on the screen? Well, embracing geography encourages us to stick around long enough to experience the fulfillment of the story. When we first relocated to Lowell, we were often lulled to sleep by the buzzing sound of the helicopter police hovering over our neighborhood in search of a fugitive, but then woke up to the nursery rhyme-themed music blaring from the speakers of the ice cream truck, along with the giggles of the lucky children who found enough money to buy a popsicle. There was violence, lots of it. When shootings occurred, we cried and mourned with our community as we faced the tragic deaths of neighbors. But we also saw our community come together to pray, host car washes to raise money for funeral expenses, and support the surviving loved ones of the now deceased. Had we not been committed to this place, we would have prematurely abandoned it before the joyous side of story was revealed, thus leaving us with the devastating narrative as our only memory.

Early in the planting process, our church was offered two different buildings. Both of them were on the other side of town and we immediately (but kindly) declined. Why? Because place matters. Any and every thing that happens inside of Highway 180, Divisadero, and

Blackstone we care about, we feel responsibility for, and we are concerned about. Do we love our entire city? Yes, of course. But those in the Lowell neighborhood are our people. This is our parish. When Emilia is walking down the street and being solicited for sex, it's OUR business. When Mary Jane's birthday was coming up it became OUR business to let the family use the church's bounce house. When Ahmad, our new neighbor, moved in and needed help transporting furniture, it became OUR business. When Jerry was murdered outside of the gas station, it was OUR business to contact the owner and demand better lighting, less alcohol advertising in the windows, and security officers on duty. When Ornela's, the new Mexican restaurant, opened it became OUR business to dine there (and our church OFTEN eats there after worship gatherings). When Bryce, the new biker, joins the local bike club and wants his bike blessed, it's OUR business. When Ashley, Dejon, Dominique, and other children playing at the neighborhood park are being negatively impacted by the scorching sun, it's OUR business to work with the City Parks Department to have a shade structure installed. Why is it our business? Because God called us to this place to help shepherd, care for, and be conduits of his transformative power in every area of life in our neighborhood. Place matters.

Barriers and Best Practices

Becoming a church that is *of* and *for* its community is not easy. This journey has led us to embrace the most complex church model we know of! It is so much easier to be a church *in* and *to* a community...sigh. However, for this generation and for our communities that model of church is not an option. Our cities are really struggling, the racial and economic divides are growing wider, and the Church cannot hide as ones who do not know what to do. We have the answer. We are the answer.

Speaking of the fulfillment of God's promises to the world, the Apostle Paul writes in Romans 8:19-20, "For the anxious longing of the creation waits eagerly for the revealing of the sons of God. For the creation was subjected to futility, not willingly, but because of Him who subjected it, in hope that the creation itself also will be set free from its slavery to corruption into the freedom of the glory of the children of God." A church movement that will pursue the difficult, complex road of embracing a relationship with their community that honors the *Imago Dei* will also discover the magnitude of God's grace along the way. Below are some considerations for churches that are feeling led to journey down this road.

Barriers to the Journey:

Everyone dances to the music they hear - It has been said that the seven last words of a church are, "We've never done it this way before." It is never an easy undertaking to ask people to do new things or to do old things in a new way. God has designed us to be habitual creatures, but sometimes these habits can serve as obstacles to obeying God. People feel most comfortable dancing to the music they can hear, which is why they struggle when visionary leadership asks them to dance to music that has not yet been released. And so leading your church to become one that is *of* and *for* the community will require the leading of God, and skilled and committed leadership, because the dominant music will do its best to draw you back into its rhythm and cadence.

Money is funny and the change is strange - Let's be honest. Multi-ethnic, multi-cultural, multi-class, intergenerational churches are what more and more people are expressing a commitment to, but in practice only a fraction of those who like the sound of them *choose* them over existing alternatives. The pursuit of being a church *of* and *for* the community is a clear strategy to increase your expenses and decrease your revenue. We have heard multiple times from generous, good-hearted people with the financial capacity to support the mission of the church that they prefer a culturally homogenous church over this more diverse model because they "work hard throughout the week and don't want to work hard at church too." For multi-ethnic, multi-cultural churches, this sentiment means that in order to fulfill the mission of the church, you may need to develop multiple streams of revenue. For On Ramps this has meant that we have shared our mission widely across the city as a means to cultivate a donor base, and we have also developed a separate nonprofit corporation that facilitates grant funding, and from which we launch social enterprises that give to the church.

Violence Violates - When your leadership expresses an interest to be a church *of* and *for* the community, it is inherently saying "As the community goes, so will we." In other words, what happens in the community affects the church. Good or bad, the church will go along for the ride and do its best to influence the journey of the community in the direction of the Kingdom of God. This means that when violence occurs in the community it will have a traumatic effect upon the church. The church will grieve and the musical worship set you planned for Sunday will have to change. And this can happen often! In response to this trauma, the church must remain faithful to its mission and rather than isolating itself from the pain it must draw nearer to it. For in doing so you afford the church and the community the opportunity to grieve together and to heal together. You become "a healing community healing its community."

Best Practices for  the Journey:

Form follows Function – There is broad agreement among most church leaders that the mission of the church is to "make disciples" (Matt 28:19). However, at church conferences and in conversations with pastors across the country who struggle with this, we consistently hear leaders confess that "Sunday morning is *not* about making disciples." Instead, it is about celebration, fellowship, or another value of the church. Consequently, many churches have created alternative, mission-centered structures to facilitate its core mission. In many cases this alternative structure is some form of small group. However, sheepishly we admit that we would view our small groups as successful if we could get 50% of our congregation to participate. Allow me to paint the picture. The church confesses that on Sunday when the majority of its membership is present we have built organizational structures that do not facilitate our core mission, and so we have created other structures to facilitate this mission at a time in which, at best, only half of our congregation might participate. To make this picture more clear, we liken it to sending our children to school five days a week only to be notified by the school that they are asking us to bring our children back on the weekends and evenings so they can educate them, because while they have been doing wonderful things with them during the day, they have not accomplishing their core mission. If you want to lead a church that is *of* and *for* its community, then you must first commit to a mission of discipling both people and your community, then build structures around that mission that will deepen and broaden it. For On Ramps this has meant a re-design of our corporate gatherings. Following the lead of Dr. Kenda Creasy-Dean's research on "Consequential Faith" (Creasy-Dean, 2010, 45), On Ramps has developed a worship gathering rhythm that facilitates our mission. Form *always* follows function.

Establish Incarnation - We have travelled the country and become great friends with pastoral leaders who have a heart for poor communities. Some of these pastors live in the communities in which they serve, and others don't. While we would never say that a church *of* and *for* the community cannot fulfill its mission if the lead pastor doesn't live in the neighborhood, we carry a strong conviction that it is a best practice. When the lead pastor lives in the community the church is serving it changes everything. It changes the topics discussed at meetings. It changes the sensitivity of the pastor to the trauma people are experiencing in their lives and neighborhoods. It ensures the church never suffers from "mission drift" because this mission has a direct impact upon the senior leader and her/his family. In addition to the senior leader living in the neighborhood, we also believe that at least 25% of the church's core leadership needs to live in the community. If only the senior leader lives in the community then this person may find him or herself in the disadvantaged position of trying to steer the ship while shouting instructions through a megaphone from a life raft in the sea. The senior leader needs the voices of other core leaders to reinforce the committed mission of the church in order to ensure the church continues to make decisions that will further this mission. As a side note, if you are part of a church that is going to transition from being *in* and *to* to being *of* and *for* the community (Sparks et al., 2014, 37–45), and your leadership does not currently live in the community, then the Christian

Community Development Association recommends that upon relocating to that community you should refrain from "fixing what you see" for at least one year, and instead spend that year developing relationships with your new neighbors and neighborhood.

Join the Tapestry of the Community - A great way for a church that is *of* and *for* the community to fulfill its mission is by becoming part of the fabric of the neighborhood in as many ways as possible. Members of your congregation should join resident groups, community-benefit organization boards that serve your community, and civic committees that impact your community. This will not only further the mission of the church but will help you gain insight into the community that otherwise would have been very difficult to capture. On Ramps has members who lead community-benefit organizations, serve on civic task forces, are members of the cultural arts community, volunteer as police chaplains, participate in the neighborhood association, and so much more.

Worship in Public Places....and Leave Evidence - On Ramps is located in the Central Valley of California which means we have a lot of good weather. Therefore, as a church that is *of* and *for* the community we move our worship gathering every fourth Saturday evening to our neighborhood park. We actually began On Ramps at this park by gathering there once each month, well before we ever gathered indoors. This may be the most important thing we have done to be seen as a church that is *of* and *for* the community. It is here that we were able to infuse peace between an estranged husband and wife. It is here that we met Malachi who was distraught after leaving his brother's hospital room, trying to cope with the pain of his brother committing suicide. We were able to comfort him and walk his entire family through the grieving process for months to come. This is the place we baptized a grandmother, daughter, and grandchildren all in the same night, and it is here where people like Johnny, Yesenia, Luis, and dozens more have given their lives to Christ. Though we only gather there once each month residents in the community who never come to our indoor gatherings say they are "part of the church that meets at the park!" Since beginning to meet at this park in 2011 we have taken ownership of it. We have formally adopted the park through our City's "Adopt-A-Park" program and have established partnerships with other churches, colleges, businesses, and city officials to rebuild the park. In only the past four years the bathrooms have been rebuilt, a condemned building has been removed, volleyball courts have been constructed, a new softball diamond was built, and the basketball courts have been resurfaced! This is evidence to the community that we are *of* and *for* it, and that God cares about this neighborhood!

Develop the Place – One of the biggest mistakes churches that are *in* and *to* a community make is that *they* decide how to engage in the healing of the community. These decisions are often made independent of any input by those whose lives are wrapped up in the community. The consequence is that churches *in* and *to* the community will either solve a problem the community doesn't think is a problem, or they will spend a lot of resources to accomplish something that is low on the priority list of the community and has very little tangible impact. An example of this was when a well-meaning entrepreneur had developed a phone system to be used to instantly deliver a recorded message to dozens of people in our neighborhood when there was a threat or suspicious person walking around. It was presented as a modern "neighborhood watch" system. While this entrepreneur meant well, it was an outside solution to a problem residents had not identified. This kind of thing happens all the time! Unfortunately for the entrepreneur, the tens of thousands of dollars he invested in this solution were lost. However, fortunately for the community, this entrepreneur was so compelled by the great people who were part of this neighborhood that he decided to move in and has been an active part of the neighborhood association ever since! This example is the type of engagement that only costs. It costs the neighborhood and it costs those outside of the community who are presenting solutions to problems residents don't identify as such. This is why a best practice for becoming a community development partner is to find the places where people gather and spend time gathering resident's thoughts about where they would like the church to engage. Places people gather often include barbershops, gas stations, liquor stores, community meetings, schools, and recreation centers. One of the best methods of gathering information from residents is through the appreciative inquiry research model. We like to ask these two questions of residents: What do you love about your community? What do you think you could change in the next six months about your community that would make the biggest difference? Often themes will emerge once you speak to enough people and these themes will guide your church's development. The reason this is a best practice for a church that is *of* and *for* the community is because it leads you to invest in people and the place where people live. This is distinct from the methodology of churches *in* and *to* the community who often develop relationships so that people will join their church. Not in the case of churches *of* and *for* their community. These churches develop their community simply because it truly is their community and because they care about its present and future.

Building Capacity in the Fresno 22

Not long after On Ramps was formed we began to meet with pastors from other high-poverty neighborhoods throughout the city. This network would gather with one common purpose: "Vision 22." Vision 22 is an ecumenical commitment to increase the capacity of inner-city churches to impact the communities they serve through sharing resources, exchanging best practices, and forging city-wide partnerships.

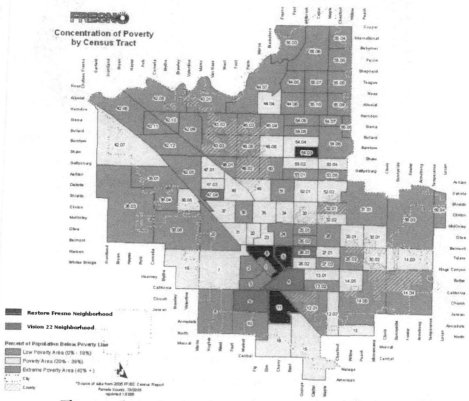

The map above visually reflects the geographic impact of Vision 22. Each of the blue neighborhoods is where the first seven of the Vision 22 churches are located. The plan in the next 12 months is to include all 22 neighborhoods of concentrated poverty in the Vision 22 network. In three of our current focus neighborhoods there are additional resources being applied through our Mayor's *Restore Fresno* Initiative, a result of the Brookings Institute's concentrated poverty study (City of Fresno, 2015).

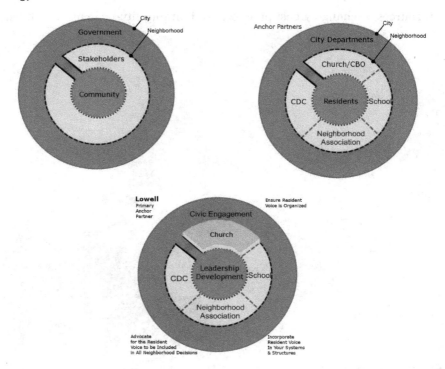

As represented by the progression of the diagrams above, each member of the Vision 22 network embraces a common understanding of the role of the church in the life of the community, and a common strategy for bringing partners and resources together for the healing of our communities. This strategy is simple. The key players in a neighborhood revitalization strategy are the community itself, other stakeholders, and the government. If you drill down further you discover that *people* make up the community, other stakeholders include churches, community-benefit organizations (CBO's), schools, housing organizations (CDC's), and a neighborhood association, and the government is made up of various departments that are responsible for different city services. All of these stakeholders are "anchor partners" to the community revitalization work. The church's role is to partner with the community to steward their vision, assist in organizing residents, ensure that the community's voice is included in every decision being made that affects that community, and convene anchor partners and government representatives when needed.

As we write, this strategy is being implemented as a best practice for church-stewarded community transformation work in Fresno's 22 neighborhoods of concentrated poverty. In each case, though the church is playing a primary role in stewarding the work, the community is driving the vision. Were we churches that are *in* and *to* the community, we would not only be stewarding the work but we would also be the authors of the vision. However, because each of these churches is *of* and *for* the communities to which we are called, we ask the residents for their vision for their community, and we simply become partners that help steward that vision until it is fully realized.

Called and Committed

So, here we are. Fully committed to this place, while fully recognizing the barriers and blessings of such a commitment. Like the distraught, broken, desperate man in our yard needing compassion from the "church people" that paradigm-shifting Sunday morning, there are others. In the summer of 2015 at one of our outdoor worship gatherings held in the neighborhood park, we met a precious woman named Grace. Grace grew up in the neighborhood and embraced many of the negative characteristics that plagued the neighborhood, and she adopted these traits as her lifestyle. She was in a gang. She sold drugs. She abused the very drugs she sold. She became a mother at a young age and lost custody of her children to the State of California's Child Protective Services. She was, to say the least, completely lost. We began walking with Grace, at her own pace. We ate together and prayed together. We spent intentional time together every Monday afternoon and swapped childhood stories. We took trips to the other side of town so she could explore, let her guard down, and relax. She surrendered her life to Jesus, was baptized at the very park we met her at, and became deeply involved in our church. Fast forward to today and Grace is no longer in a gang and is living a clean and sober life. She regained custody of two of her children and maintains regular visits with her other children. She completed her high school diploma and is enrolling to go to school for ministry. She is a leader and prayer warrior in the very neighborhood she once brought destruction to. Grace's name says it all and speaks to the goodness of God in her life and the lives of those he allows her to be a light to.

There are more families to walk with. More jobs to develop. More prayers to pray. More people to encourage. More children to tutor. More leaders to empower. More light to shine. And by being a family and a church *of* and *for* the community, we are committed to partnering with Holy Spirit to engage in the "more."

Works Cited

Berube, A., & Katz, B. (2005). *Katrina's Window: Confronting Concentrated Poverty Across America*. Retrieved February 1, 2016 from Brookings Institute Web site: http://www.brookings.edu/~/media/research/files/reports/2005/10/poverty-berube/20051012_concentratedpoverty.pdf

City of Fresno. (2015). *Restore Fresno*. Retrieved January 31, 2016 at http://www.fresno.gov/NR/rdonlyres/2E6E7C1E-5148-42EE-A2B5-BA07EDD868E1/0/RESTOREFRESNOFinalReportwithABC.pdf

Creasy-Dean, K. (2010). *Almost Christian: What the Faith of Our Teenagers is Telling the American Church*, New York: Oxford University Press.

Hawkinson, J.R., Frisk, D.C., Larsen, P.E., Larson, E., Palmquist, A.E., Sandquist, R.O. . . Engebretson, D. (2005). *Covenant Affirmations*. Retrieved June 29, 2016 at http://www.covchurch.org/resources/wp-content/uploads/sites/2/2015/03/covenant_affirmations_booklet.pdf

Hillis, D. (2014). *Cities: Battlegrounds or Playgrounds?*. Tacoma: Leadership Foundations Press.

Keller, T. (2003). *What is Common Grace?*. Retrieved December 17, 2015 at http://static1.squarespace.com/static/53189f41e4b0ee73efed7b5a/t/533ea67ce4b05289c3da94dc/1396614780413/What_Is_Common_Grace.pdf

On Ramps Covenant Church (2011). Retrieved June 19, 2016 from http://www.onrampschurch.org/#!worship/cdqh

On Ramps Economic Development Corporation (2016). Retrieved July
  27, 2016 from http://www.onrampsedc.org

Sparks, P., Soerens, T., Friesen, D.J. (2014). The New Parish, Downers
  Grove: InterVarsity Press.

Epilogue

Can Anything Good Come Out of Your City?

H. Spees

They asked it right at the beginning of his ministry, casting doubt on both Jesus and his city in one simple question: "Can anything good come out of Nazareth?" (John 1:46)

And they were asking it in their hearts at the end of his ministry, huddled there in the upper room, gripped by fear: "Could anything good come out of Jerusalem?" There was an already oppressive city ignited to violence and state-sanctioned murder when the religious and political forces joined together to crush their leader. Those forces now turned to threaten them.

Many have asked the same question of our city: "Can anything good come out of Fresno?" And you may even find yourself asking, "Can anything good come out of my city?"

There are indications, however, that the same Jesus who walked through the locked doors of the upper room to stand with that fearful band of women and men in the city that killed him is saying again to this generation, "Peace be with you!" And, as he did with them, he is showing us his hands and side, repeating, "Peace be with you," followed with a commission: "As the Father has sent me, so I am sending you."

And with that commission, a breath: "Receive the Holy Spirit." He breathes..."Ruach." The same word used only one other place in the Scripture, at the dawn of creation when the Spirit brooded and breathed over the first chaos. We can receive this commission, this breath, this new wind and be swept up into a movement that will take peace to the chaotic streets of our cities, just like it did theirs (Fortin, 2012).

Or not. We could do nothing. And we could just wallow in the stew of our negative stats or blame someone else for our city's pain...the religious right, or the religious left, the secularists or the humanists, the gangs or the judges, the President or the political parties, the economy or the culture...but in the end, we would have failed even to try, our own miniscule resources and doubtful self-assessments overwhelmed by the twenty-first century global urban challenge.

Can anything good come out of your city?

♦

In a meeting in Oslo, Norway—just after Martin Luther King, Jr. had been awarded the Nobel Peace Prize for his leadership in the civil rights movement—his father rose to make a toast. The toast was directed first to God for his blessings on the King family, and second to Martin for the honor his son had brought the King name.

But it's what happened next that caught most people by surprise.

While people were still applauding, Martin's mother rose to speak. The room suddenly fell silent, for it was only on rare occasions that Mrs. King, Sr. ever chose to speak publicly. She began somewhat softly...

> *"I want to tell you a story about myself that I'm ashamed of; it's about Martin's first public speaking venture. It was a high school debate and Martin had worked so very hard for it. In fact, he talked so well that day that everybody who heard him knew he had won. But Martin was black and the other boy was white...So, of course, the other boy won."*

At that moment, her eyes welled up with tears and her voice began to crack.

I'll never forget Martin's disappointment when he came home,"
she said; *"He was devastated! So I said to him...Martin, you're*
not going to change the world. You're just a little Negro boy."
Then sighing wistfully, she confessed:

"I was trying to keep him from what I thought could be human
heartbreak. I was afraid for him. So I did what millions of other
black mothers do all the time—we make our sons less."
Then smiling and bursting with pride, she looked at Martin and said
amidst her tears and halting speech:

"But one person can make a difference...and that's why we're
here today." (Eidsness, 2012)

♦

In every one of our cities there are wrongs that need righting,
injustices that need correcting, oppressions that need lifting, and people
who deserve better. And so we lean in. But along the way, we find
obstacles—sometimes hidden in the voice of a loved one like Martin's
mother, trying to protect us from the heartache that comes when
engaging the pain of our city. Sometimes in the resistance of institutions
reacting to our calls for change. Sometimes that voice is our own, when
we, like Martin's mother, do the wrong thing, the self-protective thing,
for the right reason, stepping back from the edge of urban engagement
because we see the cost commitment might mean to our family and those
we love. Or we see our own shortcomings which the process of seeking
the peace of our city can so powerfully unearth.

But in the end, the passion fueling Christ-Centered Civic
Transformation is the clear sense that God has called us because he
believes one person can make a difference. And what's more, he believes
that women and men working together, pursuing the peace of their cities

can, through the Spirit's power, see both individuals as well as systems and structures transformed.

For those of us co-authoring this book, the writing has given us time to reflect and the reading of each other's writing has given us opportunity to celebrate because we realize that we have been joined together to answer with one voice, "Yes, something good has come out of our city!" Our prayer for you is that you and those with you in the struggle would experience the same joy as you live into that same answer in the city you are called to love.

Works Cited

Jack Fortin, Reflections on John 20:19-23 (LF Staff Gathering, Tacoma, WA: May 23, 2012).

From a message by Rev. Joel Eidsness, Interim Pastor, First Presbyterian Church (Fresno, March 25, 2012).

Author Bios

Randy White
Executive Director of the FPU Center for Community Transformation
Randy White, (D. Min., Bakke Graduate University) is Executive Director of the *Center for Community Transformation* based at Fresno Pacific University and Seminary. He is the Founder of Pink House center for urban training that sparked a relocation movement in the city. The author of several books on community transformation he and his wife Tina live with a purpose in the Lowell Neighborhood of Fresno. They have two sons and six grandchildren.

Jacob Chao-Lun Huang
Assistant Professor of Sociology, Fresno Pacific University

Jacob Chao-Lun Huang (Ph.D. in Sociology, University of North Texas) is assistant professor of sociology at Fresno Pacific University. His interest is to process community data that community organizations can make appropriate projects for the socially marginalized residents. His research areas include aging populations, immigrants, and Asian Americans.

Monika Grasley
LifeLine Community Development Corporation
Monika immigrated from Germany as a young adult. Her passion for Asset (strength) Based Community Development comes from her own story of pain, abuse, redemption and strength. Founding director of LifeLine CDC in Merced, CA, she partners with neighborhoods to discover strengths and organize toward Shalom. She also enjoys sailing with her husband.

Phil & Rici Skei
On Ramps Covenant Church
Phil and Rici Skei (MDiv & MA Ed. Fresno Pacific) joyfully serve as Co-Pastors of On Ramps Covenant Church in the Lowell Neighborhood of Downtown Fresno. In 2006, they moved their family into the Lowell Neighborhood, once known as the "Devil's Triangle," where they model a ministry of personal and community transformation. Phil also serves as the Neighborhood Revitalization Manager for the City of Fresno. Rici is passionate about honoring the Lord through music and creative arts, and has traveled extensively leading praise and worship as well as conducting music workshops. Phil and Rici have been married since 2001 and are the proud parents of two beautiful daughters, Kadence and Kaylin.

Cathleen Lawler
Clovis Christian Church
Cathleen Lawler (DMin, Bakke Graduate University) believes that collaboration is vital in her roles in the community as a police department chaplain, hospice chaplain, neighborhood minister, and missions pastor. She also serves as a Ministry Coach for students at Fresno Pacific Biblical Seminary, and is a global mission mobilizer.

Yammilette Rodriguez
Youth Leadership Institute, Fresno
Yami Rodriquez (MA, Fresno Pacific University) is the is the Senior Director and National Trainer of Youth Leadership Institute in the Central Valley. She oversees youth-led, neighborhood policy change campaigns in Fresno County. Yami and her husband Jim are volunteer Pastors of United Faith Christian Fellowship MB where she leads advocacy work with a faith and justice lens. They have two beautiful daughters.

Bryson White
Faith in Community
Bryson White (MDiv, Fuller Seminary) and his wife Jennifer are from Fresno, California. After a fruitful period doing community organizing with the PICO group Faith in Community, he is now a PhD student at Garrett-Evangelical Theological Seminary in the field of Theology and Ethics.

HP Spees
Leadership Foundations
H Spees (DMin, Bakke Graduate University) has worked in Christian Community Development for more than 30 years in a diverse range of capacities, from establishing health clinics in Mendenhall Mississippi partnering with John Perkins, to Directing Youth for Christ, to establishing Leadership Foundations in multiple countries. He is currently advising the Fresno Mayor's Office.

INDEX

CPSIA information can be obtained
at www.ICGtesting.com
Printed in the USA
LVHW010730080822
725388LV00001B/54